Dr. Phyllis Carter writes about the "open secret" concerning pastor directed emotional, physical, and sexual abuse of their wives. Dr. Carter reveals how the church may inadvertently conspire, through habit, learned helplessness, or misinterpretation of scripture, to condone this damaging behavior. The destructive actions of misguided shepherds serve to cripple their congregations, while concomitantly destroying their families. *The Liberation of African-American Clergy Wives* is a must read from pulpit to pew and beyond.

Reverend Alfonso Wyatt
Vice President of Fund for the City of New York
Associate Minister of Greater Allen Cathedral
Jamaica, New York

Dr. Phyllis Carter lays "High Truth" on the altar. Boldly and courageously she assesses and prescribes the necessary healing for "The Liberation of African-American Clergy Wives." In the struggle for freedom if our First Ladies are not free, Who can be? A must read for clergy, first ladies, church members, mental health counselors, and all who counsel in the African-American community.

Norretta Ray, LCSW
Psychotherapist

Dr. Carter has put into words what has been kept in the dark by virtue of clergy omnipotence and lay people's need to idealize their ministries and families.

Douglass B. Clark, M. div.
Pastoral Counselor
Marriage & Family Therapist
Faculty Member, Post Graduate
Center for Mental Health
Consultant, Clark Group

Phyllis Carter has given us an "insider's" view of clergy wives that many either deny, fail to recognize, or stolidly accept. With scholarly perception and personal insight, she exposes the pain and peril of clergy households while, with compassionate balance, providing a constructive foundation for celebrating the strength and promise of clergy wives. She offers words of honesty, help, hope and healing to many who are hurting silently. This text is a must read for those who seek authentic truth and liberation in the home and the church.

Dr. John W. Kinney
Dean and Professor of Theology
Virginia Union University-School of Theology

THE LIBERATION OF AFRICAN-AMERICAN CLERGY WIVES

Empowering Clergy Wives To Experience
Emotional And Theological Wholeness

Dr. Phyllis E. Carter

"For where your treasure is
there will your heart be also." Matthew 6:21

ISBN 0-9776584-0-6

For Worldwide Distribution
Printed in the U.S.A.

Table of Contents

Dedication

I dedicate this book to my devoted husband of 42 years, Bishop Ronald H. Carter

And

My four (4) lovely daughters who I affectionately call "my flowers"
Tracy Lorette
Tanya Lynnette
Tina Louise
Tammy Lenore

Preface

The idea of this theological and psychological research grew out of the compilation of 21 years of experience revealed from my private practice as a Marriage and Family Therapist. In addition, I have spent 35 years counseling clergy wives across the country who have courageously revealed and shared their pain, confusion and injustice in the context and spiritual journey of their marriages, families, congregations and personal lives. This research is not to suggest African-American clergy wives are the only culture to experience theological and emotional deprivation in their personal lives. However, my research project was limited to one culture and ethnic group as a means of identifying statistically and demographically one group, as opposed to including several cultural groups. In addition, this research addresses other contextual variables that effect all women who are victims of domestic violence. The importance of my statistical data revealed a growing regional cross-section of clergy wives who have committed themselves to explore new talents, innovative thought patterns that direct their attention to what is relevant and contemporary.

This research has provided me with a unique and special opportunity to address and bring together, both scholarly work, and research materials, relevant to the spiritual context of the African-American community. The intent of this work is to bring about enlightenment to the body of Christ, and effective dialogue to our living the quality of a redemptive life in our families and church communities.

It is my hope to help shape, identify, and clarify the issues and annoying nemesis of domestic violence, power imbalances and mysogamistic teachings that are designed to perpetuate patriarchial power, control, manipulation and intimidation over women. My goal is to provide necessary tools to assist leaders, both, men and women to collaborate the theological premise of God's intent through His written Word, revelatory knowledge and sound doctrine, which does not include man's doctrine. It is my joy to share with my reading audience how clergy wives can address and begin to experience theological and emotional wholeness, and explore God's divine purpose in all of our lives.

Acknowledgments

I have been very fortunate to have had the help and support in the course of writing this book from family, friends, associates and well wishes. My humble beginnings started at New York Theological Seminary in New York City. When I needed to formulate my challenge and mission statement for my research project, I had the assistance of some of the finest professors to guide and assist me in writing this unique volume.

Professors: Lester Ruiz, George McClain, Barbara Austin- Lucas, Rebecca Radillo, Humberto Alfaro, Dale T. Irving, Eleanor Moody Shephard, and many others.

The members of my site team devoted much of their time and energy to assist me in the process of my research project. The members of my site team involved were: Tyra Banks, Kelly Stennett-Padmore, and William I Moore. My husband, Ronald H. Carter, has made tremendous sacrifices and support throughout my six years at New York Theological Seminary. My husband's support started in 1998 when I started the M.Div Program until its completion and remained faithful throughout my doctorate program. My journey was made possible through his intellectual and emotional support. In addition, my four daughters: Tracy Lorette, Tanya Lynette, Tina Louise and Tammy Lenore, gave me support throughout every dream, vision and educational endeavor.

I thank God for last but not least Annie Ware-Mickels who provided me with the necessary tools to make it all happen. Annie typed all of my work from 1998 throughout 2005. Her typing, editing and professionalism helped to make it all happen.

I am very grateful for Faith Printing Company for their tremendous support and encouragement for the development of this publication. Special thanks and appreciation to Juanita Barnett and Rainey Yearwood.

Foreword

Few therapists and clergy persons have dared touch the secret matters of the heart that involve African-American clergy wives. Dr. Phyllis Carter has always been a maverick in addressing tough, intimate matters of clergy families. Her new book, "The Liberation of African-American Clergy Wives" is a powerful presentation that suggests African-American Clergy wives are coming "out of the closet" of shame, pain, isolation and even segregation. Birthed out of her own history, Dr. Carter shares the plight of so many gifted, "called" and "appointed" women of clergy that have hid behind the doors of church kitchens and music departments fifty years too long. Too long have preaching women stood patiently and proudly before Sunday School classes teaching because there was no platform for preaching. Too long did wives of African-American clergy shut their eyes to known/blatant adulterous affairs often involving women of the same congregation; misuse of funds; and downright disrespect. Dr. Carter addresses these issues and many more as she graphically mirrors and I quote, "the psychic cost of ministry, including family alienation, unexpressed anger and power imbalances." She notes that there is a major shifting in the church world today. Clergy women are daring to find ways to balance money, management, ministry and marriage. The subservient role is history...there is a new woman on the scene. This is a must read for those that are not afraid of truth, confrontation and challenge.

Dr. Wanda Davis-Turner
Pastor, New Birth — West
Founder and CEO of Calling First Ladies
International, Inc.
Los Angeles, CA

This high cost of emotional exhaustion, leaves the clergy wife emotionally and psychologically depleted. Women from this patriarchal social construct tend to sacrifice their own needs for the needs of the men in their lives. This methodology allows them to overlook and minimize the reality of the open secrets.

CHAPTER ONE

The Psychic Cost of Ministry: Open Secrets

African American clergy wives across the country have maintained a perpetual silence to avoid expressing their unresolved pain and anger. Out of fear and neglect these unresolved anxieties have not been addressed. This project is designed to address the psychic cost of ministry, including family alienation, unexpressed anger and power imbalances. The power imbalances exist as a result of the patriarchal system within the church structure.

One of the clergy wives' major concerns is balancing the caring of her family and the attending to her husband with her presentation before the congregation and obligation to God. These clergy wives tend to be fearful in unveiling the hidden perils and "open secrets." An open secret is something difficult or embarrassing that affects a person, a place or thing that everyone is aware of, but nobody talks about. There are psychological realities that impact clergy wives when faced with their inability to challenge and identify life stressors. These stressors include the pain of open secrets, lack of authenticity, oppression and lack of shared power. This high cost of emotional exhaustion, leaves the clergy wife emotionally and psychologically depleted. Women from this patriarchal social construct tend to sacrifice their own needs for the needs of the men in their lives. This methodology allows them to overlook and minimize the reality of the open secrets. When burnout or breakdown occurs it is as though, they never saw it coming, because they are operating in denial. The British Navy has a single red thread that runs throughout all the rope the Navy uses. This single red thread symbolized the blood of redemption that runs throughout the Bible from the innocent animal that covered the nakedness of Adam and Eve in Genesis to the blood of the Lamb in the book of Revelations that covers the sin of the entire world. Just as the hidden red thread exists in the British Navy rope, so does the existence of agony, abuse and despair run, precariously unexplored, uninvestigated throughout the clergy wives across the country.

These "secrets" are not discussed openly, but they are known. Many of the pastors' wives are battered, others have to endure, survive and cover up for their husbands' sexual promiscuity, or their husbands' uncontrolled pornographic appetites. Some wives sleep separately from their spouses because of their husbands' bi-sexuality. Some of their husbands are homosexuals, who need wives to foster the appearance of "straightness", which their congregations demand.

As these ministers' wives gather each year at their convention, these "first ladies" of the cloth, walk the halls of their meeting place, meet for breakfast each morning, and chat over lunch. They parallel broken butterflies who want so much to live the truth of their roles, yet inside they are tormented, being deeply fearful that their terrible secret will be known. They want and need to talk but are uncertain as who to trust. The openness of the open secret is, although nothing personally is discussed, everybody has a pretty good idea that somebody is going through things similar or worse than they are and almost nobody is excluded. When one of the women is unfortunate enough to have endured public exposure and their humiliation is now public that which was secret is now public, and a new approach of compassion is thereby employed.

A clear example of the open secret will further illustrate how many of these women are blocked with fears, self-criticism, loss of identity and lack of emotional and psychological support.

Cathy (Cathy is a fictitious name) has been a Baptist clergy wife for 12 years and married for 16 years, with three children. Her major complaint came as a result of multiple extra-marital affairs committed by her pastor, priest and husband. The women that were involved in these affairs were all members of their local congregation. Cathy steadfastedly supported her husband and his dreams for a multi-faceted, mega ministry. She used all her talents, skills, and energy, to make his dream a reality. She worked in the office, sang in the choir, taught a Sunday School class, and worked with the Youth Ministry, all in the name of helping her husband. She had no idea, that her husband was sleeping with his secretary, had an affair with the organist, was seeing the Sunday School Superintendent often, and had impregnated one of the young ladies in the Youth Department and paid for her abortion. This was known by almost everybody in the church, and was "top shelf beauty parlor talk" all over town.

It appears that Cathy was the last to know the extent of her husband's involvement. Initially, she described her fears and powerlessness in her inability to confront her husband; knowing he would deny the allegations. It was interesting that she was appointed key roles in the church. She served as church administrator and director of the Women's Department and was well loved by the parishioners. They loved her enough not to share the open-secret.

We explored in therapy how these multiple roles in ministry served to compensate her pain and rejection. Cathy described how disconnected she felt from her husband, emotionally and psychologically for quite sometime. She intentionally poured her energies into her work and cared for the needs of the parishioners. It gave her purpose and false hope that the marriage would eventually get better. Cathy's family's predisposition as the oldest of five siblings reinforced her need to nurture and care for others. As the "parental child" in her family of origin, she continued the same pattern in the next generation.

After one year of therapy, Cathy made a decision, she was not responsible for her husband's indiscretions, nor was she responsible for covering up his actions by over involving herself in the ministry. She decided that it was time to let go of the open-secret, the pain and pretending life style that robbed her of her authenticity, self-esteem and empowerment possibilities. Cathy is now divorced, living at home with her children and continues to expand her gifts, talents into places that pleases her. African American clergy wives have been socialized and conditioned to sacrifice their emotional needs and repair the damage for the entire family.

One of the women indicated, "we knew it all the time", but they did, it was an open secret. Being women, there is a certain amount of caddyness involved in their group discussions. Here is where the secret part of the open secret comes from. Information is shared by women from various localities about the things they hear about each other. It doesn't have to be verified or substantiated, just information that captures the attention or imagination, about one of them.

This information can very easily be spread all over the country, quietly, secretly, without a word ever spoken to the woman involved. This is not to say that the International Conventions these women attend year after year is a gossip haven, but just as every major large building has a basement that holds its power source and provides support, so every organization has subterranean existence and this is where rumor, gossip, underhanded deals and secrets live. Briefly stated again, an open secret is knowledge unstated. The main topic of these open secrets is that there is a minister's wife being unjustifiably abused by her minister husband.

Women have had to suffer under abusive patriarchal leadership at home and in the church in an effort to secure their husband's identity and powerlessness in a racist society. This soul murder construct is executed by the patriarchal leadership that diminishes and violates women's rights and women's hope for justice. The plight of this situation being described has been able to exist as a result of the abusiveness not only these men in power, but also the lack of hope of the women who are being abused. Many of them don't know any other way to exist, therefore, they accept this as the only way there is, for example: you can't instruct someone to get up from their knees and walk, if they don't know what walking is or what walking does. The injustice of this situation, is not only the lack of justice, but also the lack of the demand for justice. In cases such as this, another scenario presents itself, when the pioneers for change in women's rights presents themselves, they are often attacked by both the culprit, in this case the abusive patriarch and the victim, (the abused sisterhood). The change the pioneer offers, is often determined to be so systemically challenging that the victims don't feel it's worth taking a chance for. Pioneers are often viewed as troublemakers, feminists, men haters and even demonically empowered lesbians. Only some sisters lurking on the shadows eventually do begin to accept what this daring pioneer has to offer, is actually their rights and have been for a long time. Someone has to take the licks, become the target. Only then will the sisters eventually stand up and join her. One by one demanding what is their justice! Justice for them, justice for their sisters and justice for their daughters.

The other side of the "secret" stems a hidden quest of the wife to find her own identity. This crucial quest by the minister's wife was aborted early on in the marital relationship when the wife committed to the emotional support of her husband and his work at the exclusion of herself. Early she mothered children that needed her hands-on care. As they developed, their autonomy rendered her maternal role less needed. Many of the wives have found that age has carried her past the flower of her youth and she is no longer the apple of her husband's eyes. She may find herself in constant competition for her husband's time, attention, conversation, affection, and intimacy. The woman, as the churches first lady, finds that the many roles she performed in the early life of the growing church can now be carried out by younger, energetic, vibrant, attractive, well educated women, who is willing and able to do what she, at one time, did single handedly.

When the ministry was young and struggling, the members were few and the finances were short, her skills, efforts, and sacrifices helped the church survive. But time has brought growth and her services are no longer required. It is during this time of displacement that the minister's wife re-enters the workforce in pursuit of a career or the educational arena, in pursuit of a degree. The age range for this role change seems to vary from 35 to 50 years of age. The difference can depend upon the amount of children involved and the size of the congregation-venturing out into another dimension of life is not so easily done. For example, in the past 50 years, pastors were not properly prepared to identify with the role of their wives, except for the wives who provided emotional support for their husbands. I had a brief conversation with a young pastor who was assigned to pastor a church in a new location. One of his concerns was addressed to his presider by asking him, what was the role of his wife in his new assignment. The presider's response was simply this, "Your wife is a member of the congregation like any woman in your church." This ambiguous response troubled the new pastor, since he thought that ministry was a partnership. His assumption came from a 20 year marriage partnership and his primary model came from his parent's marriage of over 50 years. In my experience as a clergy wife of 40 years, I have sadly observed the majority of clergy wives lacking a voice, authenticity and acknowledging shared power in their marriage. There's no clear boundaries as to the job description or expectations as to the role of the pastor's wife. The specificities of what is expected of the pastor's wife is ambiguous to say the least. She is expected to be moderately dressed, even-tempered, quietly submissive, trend setting, feminine representative of her husband, other than that she has nothing official to say or do. The only official statement she knows, is to take orders. So much has changed; so many things are not as you might remember them. Technology changes so fast, especially computers, programming, procedures, business awareness that even entry-level positions, for someone trying to re-enter the work force after fifteen (15) to twenty-five (25) years is difficult. Added to that, so many personal skills has slowed down, diminished or become obsolete. Taking the above circumstances into consideration, the reason and desire stimulating the minister's wife to return to the work force, must be stronger than the several challenges and roadblocks inhibiting the feat. Conversely, going back to school requires adjustments and efforts from the woman; she has not had to produce before. There are assignments to be returned in a timely fashion. Books have to be read and reported on, tests must be taken, classroom participation and interaction is necessary, with much younger students who are fresh out of high school and who are attuned to the up-to-date learning procedures. Re-entry into the educational arena stimulates the thinking and evaluating paraphernalia of the human kind, especially women. Education is the best vehicle of expression, the avenue to self-awareness, and deterrent of low self-esteem. Women who are able to return to school and perform well by obtaining another degree or certificate are better able to re-evaluate their hostile domestic situation. In addition, they have the ability to cultivate a better opinion of who they are, what they have to contribute and what they have the right to expect. Who they were and whatever rejection they endured was not all their fault. These ministers' wives take on a completely new aura of self-sufficiency as a result of the change in attitude, desire and determination. Whether she enters the workforce of educational arena, change is inevitable. The pain of rejection is turned into a burning desire to become something she can be proud of on her own. If she is not needed, so be it. If she is not wanted, it's time to move on; if she is not appreciated, she knows better than that. It is here that the minister's wife, who is no longer wanted, needed or appreciated, becomes vulnerable to outside attention. It is here, where this mother, who is no longer wanted by her children, who has outgrown her, no longer wanted by her husband, who has lost his passion for her, and no longer appreciated by the ministry she has nurtured to strength, that this woman is susceptible to an affair of her own. Women who launch new careers or goals usually take on a new attitude about their personal appearances. The dentist is visited to help her smile; regular appointments with her hair stylist is made and kept. New attention is paid to her feet and nails. Her weight and shape is tuned up through exercise classes and Weight Watchers. Her wardrobe is not only brought up to date, clothes usually worn by younger women now seem to be more appealing to her, because she is not so protective of the "first lady" restrictions once imposed upon her by the elder sisters of the church. She is a new self. People admiring you, and feeling good about you, begins with you admiring and feeling good about yourself. But now a man begins to smile at this charming creature, and she admittedly loves the attention. An innocent lunch at work with a co-worker or a shared assignment with a fellow student or extra help from the professor, all can become spawning grounds for an affair. Sexual indiscretions, immoral behavior, church affairs are activities men have been involved in for centuries.

The clergy wife is also struggling with the politics of: What is it and how does it work in the church structure? - "The Ole Boys Network" that intrude and prevent their family from developing a bond. The good ole boys club has done and always will cover up and protect its own from punishment and exposure. As long as they continue this cover-up, their sinful behavior will not only continue, it will be tolerated, unchallenged and expected as the norm. Clergy wives have become fearful and insecure, having lost their identity to the church. Outside sexual affairs of ministers' wives is a current day phenomenon. Whether it is a way women are using to retaliate for their husbands actions, or a means women are using for self-gratification, indications are, more women are becoming involved in sexual affairs. There is a tremendous disparity between the affairs of the men and the affairs of the women. Outside sexual affairs is not a usual activity of church-trained women, but the exception makes the rule, and there are ministers' wives who find themselves so involved. Evelyn White asserts that "abused women have a tendency to put everyone's needs before their own, because of cultural history, this conditioning in African-American women is particularly strong. These are women who hold traditional views about love, romance and relationships."[1] Women are monogamous and territorial by nature. They are satisfied with one sexual partner and are given to the task of watching over and caring for the people, the area, and the things that are hers. Women are caregivers, who are in need of intimacy, security and approval and as long as these three needs are provided for her, she will continue to provide the care and love necessary to keep her husband happy, as best as she can. The interruption and violation of her monogamous relationship or territorial privileges caused by unfaithfulness, infidelity, and insensitivity on the part of her husband can cause an aberration from her normal pattern of activity. Often, violations of this nature will bring about a vicious appetite to retaliate in kind to all that caused her pain. Evelyn White feels that most African-American men have not learned how to express their pain, frustration, lack of confidence and insecurity about his impotence in the world.[2] Men are hunters, whose basic responsibility to relationships is to protect and provide. African-American men are in constant need of approval and are stimulated by accolades. Women know this and those who have no husbands of their own can use the method of praise and adoration to the pastor to divert his attention from his wife to herself if she chooses to. Success for men can act as an

---

[1] White, Evelyn C. *Chain, Chain, Change: For Black Women in Abusive Relationships.* Seattle, Washington: Seal Press, 1985, p. 19, 22.
[2] Ibid

aphrodisiac. Success brings power and power attracts money and money creates privileges above and beyond that which is normal. That is to say, a young struggling minister, who started out with a small group of twenty-five (25) who after years of struggle and sacrifice, finds himself pasturing twenty-five hundred (2500) can be overwhelmed by the very essence of his success. This, once humble servant of the people can be consumed with himself and eventually overtaken by the spirit of entitlement. Fueled by the praise, attention and availability of younger and readily willing female participants, the husbands need to venture into sexual promiscuity, causes the lack of passion and response to his wife and partner, who has helped him carve out the success he so readily enjoys as his own. This rejection and abandonment is the prod that forces the minister's wife into new areas, new ventures and new identities.

The children of pastors (pastor's kids), have been violated by their absent fathers in the day to day family life and very often, clergy wives feel they are single parents raising their children alone. These children often face their struggles alone while their parents are busy helping others. Although other kids in the church have two sets of parents, their own plus the pastoral couple, the pastor's kids lack one set of parents for themselves. They must share their parents with an entire congregation. This "extended family" almost always includes people who adversely affect the lives of the children and the clergy family as a whole by placing heavy and unnecessary demands on their spiritual leader.

There are the whiners, the weak ones, who need daily attention if they can get it. These people drain the minister of energy, creativity, and humor that could be shared and enjoyed at home.

Then there are the stubborn, stiff-necked member of

the congregation, whose business it is to create emergencies and challenges that are time-consuming and rob the pastor, and his entire clergy family of quality time that could have been spent at home.

Of course, there are the opportunistic followers who are looking to oust the leader and take his or her place at every chance and at any cost. And when they inflict power blows upon the pastor, his wife, and children, feel the shock waves and reverberations of those blows.

Unfortunately, the pastor's children bear the brunt of these blind-sided attacks of leadership, which weaken the leader to the point of neglecting his family. For, when he gets home, he is so tired from helping and counseling, leading, fighting, and warding off attacks, that when it comes to his loved ones, their needs have to wait: "Daddy is tired."

Unfortunately, this neglect resulted in irreparable damage and a waning of love within the family. What are the dynamics of neglect, experienced by the children? What can be done? The dynamics of this type of neglect is visible when the children are pressured with unrealistic expectations to be model children and often find themselves caught in the middle of conflicts between church members and their father/pastor. They are left to deal with their struggles alone, while their parents are busy helping others. They are the innocent victims, the casualties of spiritual warfare, caught in the crossfire with nowhere to hide and no one to help.

Often PK's begin to resent the ministry because it steals their parents' time, energy, and affection. I discovered this to be true in my own family. My daughters felt like their father gave more time and energy to the church members than to them, which created a cloud of doubt and confusion in their minds as to their place in their dad's life, and left them feeling rejected and abandoned.

This seems to be a common struggle among pastor's children. Children born to parents in ministry are often unintentionally neglected and in need of validation and support. In an attempt to arrive at God's order and balance in ministry, pastors, church leaders and parents must accept the challenge to spend more time and energy to enhance the quality of life in the innocent lives of their children in ministry. In addition, they must work to change some of the destructive pressures that come with the territory of being a minister's child.

Women become frustrated, dependent, co-dependent and in need of transformation and self-change. The pastor's wife becomes alienated and oppressed in this power relationship simply because no one but another clergy wife understands her. She, very often, travels alone. She finds herself being very careful about who she shares her concerns with because of confidentiality.

In the early seventies, clergy wives were docile, subservient and accepting of their role in and out of the church. They were satisfied to dwell in the shadow of their husband, walking just behind, and feeling that they were doing what was expected. At that time, women's concerns and interest were related to making sure they were adapting to their role in and out of the home, and yet feeling overwhelmed by the daily demands of church, home, children and spouse.

In the early eighties and nineties, some clergy wives began to make a paradigm shift in their thinking and processing their personal development. Their physical and emotional exhaustion gave them an opportunity to ask questions, rethink, evaluate and address some very important concerns for the very first time. Many of these clergy wives returned to college and continued until they received an earned degree. Some wives returned to the workforce, only to learn that their jobs were more than a weekly salary, but gave them self-esteem and purpose beyond parenting and ministry. These changes caused marital conflicts with the one known as the prophet, the priest and the husband. This paradigm shift made a valuable investment into change, growth, transformation and freedom.

Although things are not the same at the home front, the clergy dyad, however, is now faced with new challenges, new and different rewards as each experience growth and development.

Clergy wives have always addressed the blatant inconsistencies and injustices that prevail in ministry, for the purpose of reconstructing an accurate framework for building wholesome lives, particularly the lives of clergy wives and their children, as they work through their developmental stages and spiritual growth and understanding. However, it lacks the notion of empowerment through the validation of self-care, and transformational possibilities. One of the critical areas faced by clergy wives is their desire to experience emotional and psychological wholeness in an effort to become their authentic selves. The clergy wife has to bear the cost of ministerial balance and stability in order to protect her family and its public image. This type of systemic imbalance places demands that the ministerial obligations be placed at a higher premium than the quality of life for the family. This imbalance is caused by the need to juggle unrealistic public demands combined with unrealistic church impositions and finally the often neglected need to fulfill their desire for relaxation and personal gratification required for being themselves. God never intended for ministerial obligations to supersede or conflict with the quality of life for clergy families. In attempt to arrive at God's order and balance in ministry, pastors, church leaders, and parents must accept the challenge to spend more time and energy to enhance the quality of life in the innocent lives of children in ministry; and along with that, they must work to change some of the destructive pressures that come with the territory of being a pastor's kid and a pastor's wife.

There needs to be a different leadership style that is representative of empowerment and transformational possibilities within the lives of clergy wives. The hierarchal vision has been shifted to a new paradigm that presents new visions and new areas that are no longer stagnant. There is a contrast from its leadership style for the past 16 years.

In chapter 2 (Power and Justice), I will reflect the significance of my work as it relates to how clergy wives can begin to challenge and explore their transformational possibilities.

Trying to create a balance between home and ministry is one of the greatest challenges in ministry today. Pastors as well as high-powered leaders from every walk of life and professions, more often than not, put their energies and priorities in the area of their jobs and, therefore, have less time and energy to devote to their wives and families. These skewed priorities deprive their wives and children of much-needed emotional support, which contribute to the nationwide rise of low self-esteem found in children of unavailable parents.

CHAPTER TWO

Power, Justice and Liberation

Historically (in some denominations only men were considered clergy), the clergyman has been the catalyst, the prophet and the priest in the African American community. However, there has been a clear distinction between his investment to his ministry and limited involvement in his home life. The major concerns are inherent in the conflict between the loyalties to God and the countervailing family ties of the "Priest." The clergy wife is left, however, with the fear of unveiling the hidden perils and politics that invade and prevent the clergy family from developing a bond.

In many instances, the family life is affected and put on hold due to role conflict and role confusion. Trying to create a balance between home and ministry is one of the greatest challenges in ministry today. Pastors as well as high-powered leaders from every walk of life and professions, more often than not, put their energies and priorities in the area of their jobs and, therefore, have less time and energy to devote to their wives and families. These skewed priorities deprive their wives and children of much-needed emotional support, which contribute to the nationwide rise of low self-esteem found in children of unavailable parents. Zipporah, the wife of Moses, faced a similar pain of alienation and isolation (Exodus 4:24-26) from her prophet, priest and husband. Apparently, Moses neglected to circumcise his son. Circumcision was an action that served as a sign of God's covenant relationship with His people as designated by God Himself. As head of the house, Moses should have performed this rite when his son was eight days old. As he is now about to become Israel's deliverer, God is displeased and vicariously uses Zipporah to do what Moses should have done.[3]

Zipporah, not only felt alone, but overwhelmed and angry that she was forced to perform a very important ritual that only the father was suppose to perform on his son. It also affected her culturally, since it was not a part of her culture. While it is true, Moses was under tremendous strain of being the leader of millions of people, a responsibility that involved his son should have merited his undivided attention. Men find time for crises, dilemmas and emergencies on their jobs. They expect the wives to hold the families together. Circumcision, however, was a divinely mandated ritual. Zipporah not only did not understand the ritual, she was not prepared to perform it, nor should have been. Her referral to Moses as a "husband of blood," was a statement brought on by the strain of the trail, and the emotional drain caused by the responsibility of performing the act. African American men see their responsibilities of leadership as being unquestioned and unchallenged duties to be performed. Wives and children see these responsibilities unfair, unsolicited and unquestionable demands thrust upon them.

---

[3] White, Evelyn C. *Chain, Chain, Change: For Black Women in Abusive Relationships.* Seattle, Washington: Seal Press, 1985, p. 19, 22.

Richard Exley describes one of the ways clergy neglects their family life is through overinvestment in their ministry. When a minister "overinvests" in his work, for an extended period of time, at least two things happen. First, he distances himself from his wife and family. The relationship that should be at the center of his being gets shoved to the ragged edge. His marriage gets the leftovers, the scraps at the end of a demanding day, hardly the stuff of which meaningful marriages are made. And when his marriage is not in good repair, it goes without saying, that he is susceptible to an affair.[4]

Some of the underlying patriarchal assumptions, symptoms and behaviors resonate in the paralyzing forces of power, control and sexism. These are forces that contaminate the home, the marital dyad and the church community. Edward P. Wimberly shares in his book:

> While African Americans inherited a more mutual form of patriarchalism, we are being influenced to adopt a more deadly form of patriarchalism that is destructive of African American females, that is, African American men are abandoning androgyny and mutuality of African patriarchalism for a model that is destructive to the growth of African American women.[5]

How and in what ways, men and women approach their myths and confusion around the powerlessness of women? Goodrich asserts some of the mystification combined with the taboo on the subject:

---

[4] Exley, Richard. *Perils of Power*: A division of Harrison House, Inc. Tulsa, Oklahoma, 1988, p. 62.
[5] Wimberly, Edward P. *Counseling African American Marriages and Families.* Louisville, Kentucky: Westminster John Knox Press, 1997, p. 8,9.

If women are powerless, how is that they sometimes seem so powerful? Confusion about this issue arises from at least two sources. One is a mystification accomplished by word-play and aimed at keeping women satisfied with their lot. Instructed that we do not really want power, we are then told that what we have actually is power. I think of such sops as the "power" of weakness, the "power" of love, the "power" of sexual surrender. The mystification, combined with the taboo on the subject of power which I mentioned earlier, makes a clear discussion of power virtually impossible.

A second source of confusion arises from transposing some private experience with social reality. A woman may be able to "get her way" with those to whom she matters through her wits, charm, or stubborn will. (Men, of course, also have this ability.) As welcome as this capacity may be to a woman, it is not the same as power. It is not power to have a headache to avoid sex. It is not power to have to nag to get heard. It is not power to have to use feminine wiles to get access to adult decision-making. What women have is personal influence akin to what a backseat driver has who can bribe, wheedle, irritate, or flirt the driver into following her instructions. This situation differs sharply from sitting in the backseat to be chauffeured, such that the right to command is overly recognized and favor overtly courted.

It is exactly in the family that women's oppression and men's power are enacted most plainly and personally. The reproduction of patriarchy occurs through family structure and family process, from who serves the coffee to who drives the car, from who pursues conversationally to who has the last word, from minor acts of deference to major decision-making. The lessons are lost on no one.[6]

Clergy wives across the country have identified their tremendous loss of power, identity and dignity within their marriage and community. Their religious convictions are supported by their scriptural reference and belief, that women must be subject to their own husbands although in contrast, scripture says, Ephesians 5:24-25 NIV[7], "men ought to love their wives, as Christ has loved the Church." This scripture also uses a metaphor indicating, as Christ loves the Church, also men ought to love their wives, sacrificially. The latter scriptural reference, however, is never enforced or challenged by clergy wives. This unilateral dictatorship within the marriage and church is designed only to perpetuate the patriarchal systems for the purpose of neutralizing women to accept their plight of oppression. Unfortunately, most African American male leadership sanctions rigid role models and utilizes scripture to support stereotypical and hierarchical roles as a means of unilateral power and control. Clergy wives end up feeling that whatever goes wrong in the marriage and family is her fault and that it is her responsibility to correct this vicious cycle. This keeps her husband feeling safe, secure and unresponsive to her needs.

How can women continue to strive and survive without a voice, without an audience and without a community that addresses her needs and pain? Judith Myers Avis addressed power politics in therapy with women, when she makes a

---

[6] Goodrich, Thelma Jean. *Women and Power: Perspectives for Family Therapy.* W. W. Norton & Company, New York, 1991, p.10.
[7] *Holy Bible, NIV*

critical distinction between feeling powerful and having power. She says we must not confuse the process of helping women to claim and exercise a greater degree of personal choice with the process of helping them to actually have power either in their family relationships or in the outside world. She further elaborates that the process of empowering women therapeutically cannot adequately be summarized with a list of interventions. Empowerment is a holistic process which involves comprehensive integration such as:

- Political understanding of the oppression of women
- A high degree of respect, their strengths and their wisdom
- An understanding of change, individual family, and her larger system[8]

This type of therapeutic process can be an opportunity not only for women to address their issues that bring them to a counseling situation, but the therapist must be able to make the appropriate connection and assessment with women who feel powerless, battered and hopeless.

The harmful implications and consequences of this type of injustice in the religious community can no longer be tolerated, glossed over, or minimized. Psychologically and emotionally, clergy wives are left betrayed, confused, and ambivalent by their husbands' theological and moral justification of their action and behavior. Clergy wives end up not only being betrayed by their husbands, but equally feel betrayed by God as well.

How and in what ways does the patriarchal system condition women to accept their oppression, when

---

[8] Goodrich, Thelma Jean. *Women and Power: Perspectives for Family Therapy.* New York: W.W. Norton and Company, 1991, p. 199.

historically, spirituality and religion has been the catalyst for their survival? Evelyn C. White reports "Because of institutionalized and individual racism in American society, Black men, in particular, have experienced much of the powerlessness, low self-esteem, feelings of ineffectiveness and insecurity that characterize many abusive men."[9]

Knox (1985)[10] states that spirituality is deeply embedded in the Black psyche. Nobles (1980)[11] demonstrated that this sense of spirituality has its roots in the tradition of African-American religions. Religion has always played an integral part of African Americans. It has accompanied the individual from conception too long after death.

Cheryl Gilkes describes one of the ways African American women have internalized their guilt by ignoring their own needs for self-development and care for self in an attempt to wage war on behalf of African American men. She offers valuable reasons how the African American women are very vulnerable to abuse and exploitation because of the internalization of gender norms of wider society.[12] I agree with Edward P. Wimberly who asserts how abuse and victimization often leads to self-abuse where one learns self-hatred and sacrificing one's self-growth. This kind of abuse can be perpetrated by either men or women. However, in a patriarchal oriented society, male abuse of females is more prevalent.[13]

[9] White, Evelyn C. *Chain, Chain Change: For Black Women in Abusive Relationships*. Seattle, Washington: Seal Press, 1985, p. 20.

[10] Knox, D. H. *Spirituality: A Tool in the Assessment and Treatment of Black Alcoholics and Their Families. Alcoholism Treatment Quarterly.* (2 (3/4) 1985, p. 31-44.

[11] Nobles, W. W. *Africanity: Its Role in Black Families. The Black Scholar.* New York: Harper and Row, 1980, p. 10-17.

[12] Gilkes, Cheryl, *"The Loves' and Troubles' of African-American Women's Bodies: The Womanist Challenge to Cultural Humilation and Community Ambivilance.* Maryknoll, New York: Orbis Books, 1993, p. 240-41

[13] Wimberly, Edward P. *Counseling African American Marriages and Families.* Louisville, Kentucky: Westminister John Knox Press, 1997, p. 71.

The Black man may decide that if nothing else, he will at least control what happens in his home and within his family. He may behave abusively because, like most men, he has not learned how to express his pain, frustration, lack of confidence and insecurity about his importance in the world. But abusing those he loves only serves to make him feel worse, not better, about himself. For he has confirmed the racist stereotype about the violent nature of Black men. He may come to believe that he deserves to be feared as much as society fears him.

In addition to the control that he asserts in his home, he creates another world in the church community as well. As pastor, priest, and husband, he produces a place of power and domination in an effort to cover his ineffectiveness and psychological impotence. How is this mass soul murder executed and how is it possible that thousands of women remain non-responsive and voiceless in a community that provides faith, hope and social mobility? Soul murder is a raping of the mental, emotional and spiritual esteem of an individual. Mental esteem has to do with the ability to think, plan, and determine in ones own behalf. Emotional esteem has to do with the ability to respect, mobilize and desire all things that are good for ones self. Spiritual covenant relationship with Almighty God as described in His Word and felt in the spirit.

Women have had to suffer under abusive patriarchal leadership at home and in the church in an effort to secure their husband's identity and powerlessness in a racist society. This soul murder construct is executed by the patriarchal leadership that diminishes and violates women's rights and women's hope for justice. The plight of this situation being described has been able to exist as a result of the abusiveness not only these men in power, but also the lack of hope of the women who are being abused. Many of them don't know any other way to exist, therefore, they accept this as the only way there is. Example: you can't instruct someone to get up from their knees and walk, if they don't know what walking is or what walking does. The injustice of this situation, therefore, is not only the lack of justice, but also the lack of the demand for justice. In cases such as this, another scenario presents itself, when the pioneers for change in women's rights presents themselves, they are often attacked by both the culprit, in this case the abusive patriarch and the victim, (the abused sisterhood). The change the pioneer offers, is often determined to be so systemically, challenging that the victims don't feel its worth taking a chance for. Pioneers are often viewed as troublemakers, feminists, men haters and even empowered lesbians. Only some sisters lurking on the shadows eventually do begin to accept what this daring pioneer has to offer, is actually their rights and have been for a long time. Someone has to take the licks, and become the target. Only then will the sisters eventually stand up and join her. One by one demanding what is their justice! Justice for them, justice for their sisters and justice for their daughters.

What is justice? It is the administration of what is just and fair. It is the action, practice or obligation of awarding each his/her just do. Classically, the concept of each person receiving what is due. Biblically, the emphasis is on right relationships and persons receiving a share of the resources of the society. Concern is expressed for the oppressed and their right treatment. Justice is related to love and grace. Social justice is the recognition of the rights and obligations of individuals and a society. Full participation in the institutions and processes of society is a goal. Exclusion and marginalization become forms of social injustice.[14]

---

[14] McKim, Donald K. *Westminster Dictionary of Theological Terms*. Louisville, Kentucky: Westminster John Knox Press, 1996, p. 152.

How Can Women Become Empowered

How can women become empowered? How can women begin to face a celebrated life of justice, liberation and shared power? Empowerment is a relational word, a relational action frequently heard in the women's movement, the term usually designated a benevolent but unilateral transaction in which one person enhances another's ability to feel competent and take action, that is, enhances another's power-to. Typically, women have the ability to empower others, to move others to action.[15] This ability rests on personal authenticity. Listening and responding from the heart creates emotional connection and releases energy. For each person in a conversation to give the other this quality of attending leads each one to increased self-worth, zest, knowledge, energy for the action, and desire for more connection.

Reading Bell Hooks book entitled: "Yearning," has allowed me to revisit my own domination and oppression. My revolt comes from Black male dominance and oppression from my former church organizational experience of 40 years. My struggles became a reality when the oppressed (men/women) became my oppressor, when I left the oppressed traditional church setting. This Black political thinking continues to exist when Black men continue to assume dominant leadership roles.

Bell Hooks social location and memories of childhood has made a tremendous impact on her disciplining knowledge. In her book, "Wounds of Passion", she informs her readers of her continual struggle for her own work, and the desire for radical social change and social justice. Bell Hooks designs a methodological construct to neutralize the

---

[15] Goodrich, Thelma Jean. *Women and Power: Perspectives for Family Therapy*. New York: W. W. Norton & Co. Inc., 1991, p. 20

White supremacist consumer market by educating the Black community of their history, and awakening the Blacks to criticism consciousness. Her practice involves purpose, identity and effect. I believe her struggle will continue to affect her community through storytelling and facts about the African-American past. As an African American woman, ordained minister, pastor and marriage and family therapist, I am affected by the same methodological construct to liberate, authenticate and celebrate my Black community. I intend to continue to wage war against racism, sexism and cultural imperialism[16]. As I teach, preach, pastor and counsel my community, I dare not loose my intensity, passion and fire as we strive for solidarity and coalition. I see myself as one of the women Bell Hooks speaks about, "making home a community, a place of resistance, shared by women globally."

It is my hope, reality and vision that global ministry will begin to address liberation and justice for the African American clergy wives across the country. It is my call to ministry that, hopefully, will affect the wholistic needs of the African American community as it relates to my initiative of change to promote healing and restoration in the body of Christ. Basic to an effective program would require a sensitivity and the challenge to address and embrace race, class and gender which are basic forces that impact our every day lives. Every fiber of the African American community is impacted by the loss of hope and absence of meaning and social frustration. In an effort to meet the needs of its constituency, the church community should work toward promoting healthy personality development and satisfactory social functioning as it relates to the multiplicity of various

---

[16] Hooks, Bell. *Yearning: Race, Gender, and Cultural Politics*: Boston, MA: South End Press, 1994, p. 46.

family members, both individually and collectively.

It is these concerns that "fit" into the framework of my ministry to liberate clergy wives throughout the country in an effort to bring justice in our homes, justice in our churches, and justice throughout our communities. This framework of ministry will be a means of reaching out through the intervention of workshops, seminars and a collaborative effort through a forum of care providers, psychologists, social workers, marriage and family therapist and clergy. This forum would be designed to address issues relating to the development of gender diversity, class diversity and justice. This therapeutic process would include a representation of professionals to form a Christian coalition to assess all possibilities around the forces of race, gender and class in Black America. Historically, the church has always been the catalyst in the Black church that addresses those paralyzing forces, in order to bring hope, faith and social mobility in the Black community.

Although I have limited this research project to the African American community, this study, however, does not suggest that clergy wives bashings only exist in the African American community. A recent article from London indicated a two-year study revealing shocking evidence to domestic violence by clergymen. Research by an Edinburgh University divinity scholar found many clergymen's wives had suffered mental, physical and sexual abuse. Lesley Mac Donald interviewed 23 women as part of her investigation into violence against women in the church which she believes is a result of a misuse of power by clergymen. She studied cases involving abuse within church marriages as well as clergy abuse of women from outside the church who had sought church advice in a counseling context. One woman, now divorced from her minister husband, told her: "I really thought he was going to do a mastectomy one night and I got very, very deep scratches on my breast and I went to my doctor." "One time he punched me and gave me a black eye and I wasn't allowed to go out until the black eye got better." He told the family I had walked into a cupboard door."[17]

As a Black professional woman in the community, I am experiencing the male indifference to Black women becoming a competitive edge and threat to their husbands' ministry, which has always been faced with trepidation regarding equal roles in the ministry. Bell Hooks, in her book entitled, "Teaching to Transgress", (1994), she makes a poignant reality that she was stunned that in search of scholarly material, she could not find any focus on gender difference in Black life. Her concern was that scholars usually talked about Black experience, when they were really talking about Black male experience. Since writing her book in 1994, I would imagine a shift in the right direction is taking place in some areas. In recent years, my growing awareness and sensitivity is committed to accepting the challenges that impact Black life, as it relates to class difference, race, gender and justice. As a result of my personal experience and exposure within my private practice (21 years) and broad experiences both ecumenical and interdenominational, I have been able to define, respond and confront to various class differences when necessary.

It is a tremendous opportunity to serve my community, serve my fellow citizen in a way that promotes respect, dignity, and individuality to those that I serve, regardless of race, gender and class. In ministry, each "fit" uniquely and respectfully as God's ambassadors.

---

[17] MacDonald, Lesley. "Clergy Wives Tell of Bashings." Surry Hills, Australia: _Daily Telegraph_, 1997.

Marie M. Fortune gives some insight by providing an ethical framework. She suggest that the religious community should act in the face of injustice, rather than remain passive and uninvolved. Secondly, people need to take violations of integrity seriously. Thirdly, relationships between and among people are a primary value. We must begin with the lived experiences of people, and take the side of the powerless and victimized.

Micah's admonition (6:8) NIV[18] to do justice and mercy and to walk quietly with God most clearly summarizes the church's responsibility to its people, to their families, and to their wives in an attempt to restore right relations.[19]

As I continue to embrace and serve my community, my focus and passion for ministry is to uphold the principles of power and justice as well as Theological and Ethical issues in the body of Christ. In the following chapter, I will address some of the stereotypical embedded theological issues that have affected African American marriages, and their families. These forces have been influenced by stereotypical strict sex roles and power imbalances as a result of the patriarchal system. To experience shared power, God has always intended for men and women to move from oppression to emancipation.

---

[18] _Holy Bible, NIV_
[19] Fortune, Marie M. _Is Nothing Sacred? The Story of a Pastor, the Women He Sexually Abused, and the Congregation He Nearly Destroyed._ United Church Press, Cleveland, Ohio: 1998, p. 112-113.

Fundamentally, and historically, African American women have been conditioned to accept their plight and their reality. They are conditioned to solemnly pledge their promise and loyalty to the cause of their family and their man, in the midst of difficult and perplexing situations. Although abuse has been accepted throughout history and exists in all societies, the impact of rigid sex roles have contributed to the social acceptance of emotional, mental and physical battering.

CHAPTER THREE

The Theological/Ethical Discourses:

There needs to be a theological shift in the clergy marital relationship, a shift that speaks to the level of freedom that each spouse is free to expand, explore, grow and experience their full potential and possibilities. The essential idea is to create and cultivate equality and respect instead of surviving in an oppressive, subjected and sexually violated relationship. A Christian and loving marital relationship cannot thrive in a subordinate and controlling environment, due to the fact that subordination is a tool that enforces power, control, manipulation and abuse. These forces are not theologically or ethically sound.

Black women tend to sympathize with their husbands as a result of the same racist society that they both suffer and live through. Evelyn White states in her book:

We know that the Black family has been damaged by slavery, lynchings and systematized social, economics and educational discrimination.[20]

As a result of this emotional turmoil and imbalance in

[20] White, Evelyn C. *Chain, Chain, Change: For Black Women in Abusive Relationships,* Seattle, Washington: Seal Press, 1985, p. 22.

the clergy marital relationship, there needs to be positive energy generated towards changing strong, culturally supported patterns of behavior.[21] This process requires cultural changes, new attitudes and Black theology that focuses its attention on liberation and reconciliation.

How can clergy wives be free to expand, explore and grow in an atmosphere of control, manipulation and abuse? Does The Almighty address stereotypical roles of males and females in selected traditions? How can couples and families move toward a functional understanding of roles in terms of their utility functions for the sake of the marriage or family rather than for the sake of the role itself?[22]

Linda L. Ammons reveals the plight of Black battered women. She asserts that African-American women depend on informal networks and seek support through prayer, personal spirituality, and the clergy. The African-American church is a traditional source of strength. Pastors (typically male), are a central authority figure in many black communities. However, misinformed ministers may overemphasize the value placed on suffering as a test from God. Further, some clergy have misconstrued biblical principles of love, forgiveness and submission to reinforce sexism and subordination, which can be used to justify abuse. Black female parishioners are often told from the pulpit to protect the black male because he is an endangered species.[23]

Fundamentally, and historically, African American women have been conditioned to accept their plight and their reality. They are conditioned to solemnly pledge their promise and loyalty to the cause of their family and their

---

[21] Ibid

[22] Wimberly, Edward P., *Counseling African American Marriages and Families*, Louisville, Kentucky: Westminster John Knox Press, 1997, p. 20.

[23] Ammons, Linda L. "Babies, Bath Water, Racial Imagery and Stereotypes: The African-American Woman and the Battered Woman Syndrome." Law Review 1003-1004. 1995.

man, in the midst of difficult and perplexing situations. Although abuse has been accepted throughout history and exists in all societies, the impact of rigid sex roles have contributed to the social acceptance of emotional, mental and physical battering. This social acceptance has been evidenced by aggression, competitiveness, power and stoicism.[24] Evelyn White asserts how even after the changes brought about by the women's movement, these attitudes and expectations about masculinity remain very strong. Rare is the parent who really expects a male child to wash dishes or vacuum or who encourages him to pursue a career as a nurse or librarian, because those are considered "women's jobs" (and therefore have lower status and lower pay). Equally rare is the parent who really expects a female child to take out the garbage or mow the lawn or to study physics and become an aerospace engineer. As girls, and then as women, we are expected to be submissive, dependent, passive, indecisive, weak and emotional in this society.

As a result of this strict sex-role stereotyping, both men and women are constrained when they attempt to express their full range of emotions and abilities. A woman who demonstrates too many "masculine" characteristics is very likely to be called unfeminine or headstrong or a lesbian. A man who speaks softly or interacts with others unaggressively may be called effeminate or weak. If he enjoys or pursues a career in fashion, opera, music or dance, he may be presumed homosexual because those professions emphasize grace, beauty and sensitivity.[25]

Kroeger and Beck, authors of *Women, Abuse, and The*

---

[24] White, Evelyn C. *Chain, Chain, Change. For Black Women in Abusive Relationship:* Seattle, Washington: Seal Press, 1985, p. 9.
[25] White, Evelyn C. *Chain, Chain, Change. For Black Women in Abusive Relationship:* Seattle, Washington: Seal Press, 1985, p. 9.

Bible[26] state that many religious institutions believe that "God intends that men dominate and women submit."

Moving from oppression to emancipation is what God intends for a godly marriage, in an effort to experience shared power from subordination to liberation and freedom to grow as a couple and individuals. Ruth Dearing exegetes the formation of Eve in Genesis 2:22. She asserts this equality of the sexes is made plain in the formation of Eve. In Genesis 2:22 we read, "The Lord God made [*builded He into,* Hebrew] a woman from the rib He had taken out of the man, and He brought her to the man." (NIV). Matthew Henry expresses this equality very beautifully when he says,

> The woman was made *of a rib out of the side of Adam;* not made out of his head to rule over her, nor out of his feet to be trampled upon by him, but out of his side to be equal with him, under his arm to be protected, and near his heart to be beloved.

Woman was thus of the same nature as man, of the same flesh and blood, and of the same constitution in all respects.

The ability to nurture and cultivate shared power in marital relationships has been for some obsolete and for others almost non existent. The avoidance of shared power in the marital dyad has created a context around boundary issues. Nancy Boyd-Franklin says that boundary issues are complex in African American families. Boundaries define who participates in the family and how.[27] In the African American community, if the husband takes the lead without conversation and negotiation, then the imbalance fosters

---

[26] Catherine Clark Kroeger and James R. Beck. *Women, Abuse, and The Bible: How Scripture Can be Used to Hurt or Heal*, Grand Rapids, Michigan: Baker Books, 1996, p. 16.
[27] Boyd-Franklin, Nancy. *Black Families in Therapy: A Multisystems Approach,* New York: Guilford Press, 1989, p. 65.

control and domination and oppression as a lifestyle.

It is my understanding that God intended that each family member should live their lives in ways that liberate their growth and development. In other words, The Creator's goal for each other is for couples to take responsibility to nurture and celebrate each other's potential and goals to the extent of their success.

In the past 25 years, I have observed a plethora of clergy wives throughout the country experiencing the high cost of emotional exhaustion and pain they have had to endure due to "ministry." However, I believe that God never intended ministry to be in conflict with marriage. What remains constant in society and church is the strong presence of power imbalances as a result of the patriarchal system within the church structure. Lettie L. Lockhart states in her book, *Spousal Violence: A Cross Racial Perspective,* that:

The major cause of African American male violence toward their spouses was jealousy. Moreover, it was found that shared decision making and equalitarian spousal relationship fostered less violence then the traditional and patriarchal style of spousal relationships. Sex role socialization in the home environment is also a contributing factor to violence against women.[28]

Many African American clergy wives from various denominations have expressed to me their futile attempts to strive for some type of normalcy to exist in their marriages. Their present state and future were viewed as a diminished hope from the past and their lives were spent waiting for hope to rise, and it never did. How can hope rise in a unilateral relationship void of shared power, disrespect and

---

[28] Lockhart, Lettie L. *Spousal Violence: A Cross Racial Perspective in Black Family Violence*. Lexington, Massachusetts: In Robert L. Hampton (Ed.). 1991, p. 85-101.

dignity? Only when women are allowed to rise to their full potential can they hope for equality. Accordingly, the real challenge is for a shift in male Christian thinking, from "Me-ism" to "We-ism," for only teamwork can make the equality dream, work.

In 1995, Christianity Today published the stories and reactions of three women whose pastor, priest and husband were engaged in ministry and also engaged in adulterous relationships that destroyed their marriages. Parts of the country were involved in churches spanning the ecclesiastical spectrum, from fundamentalist to mainline, but they shared the same experience of a tragically disrupted life. One of the women described her husband, priest and pastor guilty of betrayal and infidelity after a 32 year ministry within a large denomination. She felt trapped, trying to balance responsibilities in the home and church while struggling to maintain a façade of normality within a disintegrating marriage. In her closing statement, she states:

> "At the time of the divorce, I was 60 years old. I then worked full-time for several years until retirement. I have very little money and often wonder what will happen to me in the future. I never prepared for a career of my own. My career was to be a mother and a pastor's wife, with all that this use to mean."

Janet has strong feelings about churches and denominations that permit men who have been unfaithful to continue in pastoral ministry. She believes that some of them will be unfaithful again. She wonders about the invisible aftermath of their behavior –how it has hurt people, especially those whose faith in God has been shattered.[29]

---

[29] Sanderson Streeter, Carole. "Whatever Happened to His Wife." _Christianity Today_, 3 April 1995. V. 39.

What are the theological concerns that impact the lives of African American marriages and their families? What are the themes, values and emphases that maintain distinctiveness and uniqueness with regard to their marriage and family?

Anderson J. Franklin suggests one key factor in African American marital and family concerns is the relationship of racial oppression and the manhood issues of African American men. One response of African American men to racism is compulsive masculinity. Here compulsive masculinity refers to males adopting norms of toughness, emotional detachment, sexual conquest, manipulation, and thrill seeking as a response to economic marginality and racial discrimination.[30] In compulsive masculinity the worldview is present-oriented and attaches no value to work, sacrifice, self-improvement, or service to family, friends, or community. The compulsive masculinity factor plays a significant role in many of the problems that I encounter working with African American couples and families. Often, protecting the African American male ego is a major component that cannot be ignored when doing pastoral counseling with African American males and females.

While African American men respond to racism with compulsive masculinity, a characteristic response of an African American woman to racism is the internalization of self-hatred. This is manifested through allowing herself to be blamed by society and black men for the ills of the African American community. She extends herself for the concerns of the community at the expense of herself. She is often an over-functioner taking on more than her share of the workload in families, and she uses a variety of self-destructive

---

[30] Franklin, Anderson J. *Therapy With African American Men: Families in Society* 73 *(June 1992): 351*

means to hold on to her man, including taking on more of the financial burden. This is internalized racism, because she takes problems on that she neither created nor can solve.

Due to the conflict experienced by African American women's response to oppression and racism, she internalizes self-hatred and denial. This oppression is manifested by allowing herself to be blamed by society and her prophet, priest and husband for the tragedy of the African American community. African American women often become overachievers and overextending themselves by taking on the cares and concerns of the church community, in an effort to hold on to her unavailable husband.

Wimberly suggests African American women use a variety of self-destructive means to hold on to their man, including taking on more of the financial burden.[31] The average clergy wife typically enables her husband in an attempt to cover up his avoidance towards her and the family. Her need to protect him in the eyes of their children and the church they serve has become her preoccupation and priority. As a result, her greatest quest is for public success and public approval for her husband's ministry. But too often, keeping up this "superwoman" image requires her to sacrifice her own needs, and her own identity gets lost in the shuffle. Kevin Cashman defines identity as our identity and purpose only in terms of external results; the circumstances of our lives define us. In this external driven state of identity, life is fragile, vulnerable, and at risk. And everything that happens to use defines who we are.

The conflict raging within the reality of the Afro-American clergy wife is layered with concerns for everyone, and everything but herself. She must be concerned for her

[31] Wimberly, Edward P. *Counseling African-American Marriages and Families:* Louisville, KY: Westminster John Knox Press. 1979, p. 71.

husband, his success, his career, and his public image. In so doing, she must also cover his private problems, for the church, and the public, and they are often many. She must next be concerned for her children. She must try to protect them from the often overbearing scrutinous demands the congregation places upon them. Then she must try to protect them from the often lopsided attention their father receives, as to what he gives in return. She must control and explain to their children that they are indeed loved, but their father must be loved, respected, revered and protected at all times, because he is a pastor. Then, she must thirdly be concerned about the church she worships in. She must maintain a persona of wife/mother/first lady, never-ruffled, ever-smiling, unwavering all-knowing, understanding woman of God. She must also find room in her heart to love God. There is very little time, room or energy for herself. But what if she is equipped with a gift, or a skill? What if there is an inner ability within her, to do even more then the basic minister's wife requires?

Debbie Warhola wrote an article giving the flipside of the new clergy wife who represents the 90's as independent-minded yet supportive. The 90's clergy wife does not fit a certain mold, fulfill certain expectations, or adhere to a certain role. Although the women still face some long-held expectations, their lives are less bound by convention, and they have more freedom to choose their own paths. When she decides not to live her life fully according to others' expectations, the stereotypes often disappear. All in all, it's a difficult role, wives say, one that can make them feel like they're swimming upstream with an open-mouthed whale close behind.[32]

---

[32] Warhola, Debbie. "Clergymen's Wife of the 90's is Independent-Minded Yet Supportive." _Knight Ridder/Tribune News Service_. 27 March 1996, p. 327, k 0550.

Cashman's book on, "leadership from the inside out" involves awakening our inner, our identity, purpose, and vision that our lives thereafter are dedicated to a conscious intentional manner of living.[33] Kevin Cashman articulates leadership formation by suggesting that leadership is not simply something we do, it comes from somewhere inside us. Leadership is a process, an intimate expression of who we are. It is our being in action. Our being, our personhood says as much about us as a leader as the act of leading itself.[34] Cashman further describes that leadership is authentic self-expression that creates value. Anyone who is authentically self-expressing and creating value is leading. Authenticity requires a life long commitment to self-discovery and self-observation.

African American wives need to begin to challenge and question their own authenticity or the lack of it. If authenticity is for all humanity, why are women oppressed and men revered? When did ministry become greater than a person's authenticity?

When clergy wives begin to become more authentic, have a voice, and develop effective ways to communicate their concerns, they will begin to consider the notion of moving from an embedded theology to a deliberative theology. Embedded theology has reference to theological messages from our church tradition and experiences that have been bred into the hearts and minds of the faithful since our entry into the church. The embedded theology is what we carry around with us from our tradition. Deliberative Theology reflects questions what had been taken for granted. It inspects a range of alternative understandings in search of that which

[33] Cashman, Kevin. *Leadership from the Inside Out: Becoming a Leader for Life.* Provo, UT: Executive Excellence Publishing, 1998, p. 22.
[34] ibid

is most satisfactory and seeks to formulate the meaning of faith as clearly and coherently as possible. Like Solomon, the theologian wants to take all the testimony and evidence under advisement, press beneath the surface to the heart of the matter, and develop an understanding of the issue that seems capable – at least for the present – of withstanding any further appeal. This is deliberative theological thinking.[35]

Christianity today reported the divorce action, in which Carol Graham alleged that her husband (Billy Graham's youngest son) not only abused drugs and alcohol and had inappropriate relations with other women, but also engaged in domestic violence and used pornography frequently. Despite the turmoil, Ned Graham carries on the ministry of East Gates with the expectation of launching new training projects in China. Ned Graham continues as East Gates president. Since the divorce, Carol Graham has returned to full-time work as a nurse. She tells Christianity Today, "I am a middle-aged woman and the reality is, I have nothing. I had an agenda: I wanted to be happily married and wanted to be a family. It just didn't work out that way. I recognized that God is working His best out for my life.[36]"

In the context of my own clarion voice, I intend to encourage African American clergy wives across the country to claim and accept the challenges to examine, articulate and interpret their faith from daily encounters with their God and their Christianity. This type of exposure will sensitize African American women to also examine the future of the African American marriages and families upon their lives. As a clergy wife for the past 40 years, I have gained a broader theological perspective as I shifted from my former

[35] Howard W. Stone and James O. Duke. *How To Think Theologically*. Minneapolis: Fortress Press, 1996, p. 23.
[36] Carnes, Tony. "Ned Graham's Woes Shake East Gates Ministries." _Christianity Today_, 1999. 43 No 14 26 D6.

embedded theology to a selective deliberative theology. This awareness has been both redemptive and rewarding.

My present working theology has further developed my faith in an attempt to seek a deeper understanding about God and His will for my life and the life of others. It has also been a reflection of lived realities that has had the capacity to impose and challenge every area of my life. It is in the context of my own clarion voice that I speak to my tradition, my faith and my God. This exposure has sensitized and broadened my frame of reference that speaks to my present struggle for social justice as I contemplate and wrestle for answers from a loving and compassionate God. God's actions, from my vantage point and experience, reveals God's restorative and reconciliation to humanity as He transforms and empowers lives throughout their broken and shattered relationships throughout the body of Christ.

Theological Question

How can African American clergy families, of today enhance the quality of life in the presence of dysfunctional, traditional and cultural barriers that stifle growth and potential in our families?

As a clinician, I feel there needs to be a broader sensitivity throughout the spiritual and religious community that will present an initiative of change and creativity that will address family survival awareness and strategy techniques to prove sustenance for families in crises. For example, Dr. Betty Shabazz has risen from the ashes of personal despair to become a depositor of good, an example of positive accomplishments, an icon of success, for everyone and indeed anyone who seeks a reason to go no further when life has dealt them a sure losing hand. How can these things be? Why should something as dreadful as death befall someone who has already suffered so much? But most of all, at the hand of someone from whom you expect love – a member of your family. Agonizingly, why did this happen?

In the Gospel of John, the 9th chapter, Jesus and His disciples came across a situation that provokes a theological question. A man born blind from birth sits by the wayside. Jesus' disciples ask the question, who sinned, this man or his parents. Obviously, some evil was committed by someone, it's certainly not fair for someone to have to spend their life in total darkness without evil being the root cause for it. There seems to be, in all humankind, a need to know. The ability to rationalize an understandable, explainable verdict of guilt or innocence. As the disciples traveled with Jesus, they were being trained for the responsibility of introducing the world to a completely new sphere of life called Christianity, a new organism called the church. In their quest for knowledge, they inquired of each situation they encountered. Situations that heretofore had been passed by as part of life. Poverty, sickness, paralysis, leprosy, blindness was as much a part of daily life as were the dusty roads upon which they had to travel. Yet how, the disciples wanted explanations from their leader, who seemingly had an answer to everything. Why did this man come from the womb blind? Was it something he did, or can the fault be laid at the feet of the parents? If wrong caused the impediment, then the cause is sin. If sin is involved what process of salvation can be applied to resolve the matter? What is the condition of sin and salvation in the death of Dr. Shabazz? Is an emotionally imbalanced grandson the product of sin, or can we call the condition sin itself. If emotionally distressed individuals are categorized as sinful then who caused it? Why did it have to happen, did something his mother did, or did not do cause this condition, and did his mother completely explain the extent of his condition. Did Dr. Shabazz understand her grandson's condition, and disregard it as not harmful, or perhaps she was completely aware of it, and in a moment of repose was caught off guard.

All of these hypothetical, theoretical questions still leave a question in the mind of the inquisitive – why? Lord, why did this terrible thing happen, when your omnipotence could have prevented it and spared us all the strain of searching for answers and resolve. Then, from somewhere in the abyss that is filled with unanswered questions, another question comes forth to challenge the strength and tenor of our wisdom. WHY NOT! Who says life in this world would be comfortable, uncomplicated, and understandable. The response to the question, although positive, was in and of itself, complicated. A miracle of sight was eventually accomplished by a soliloquy of answers and activity. When an answer is in compound form, time and activity are galvanized by obedient participation. Jesus answered his disciples by saying neither the parents or the man was guilty of sin. This drama was arranged sometime in the unknowable future, all-knowing God the Father, who set it up, so that His son, Jesus the Christ might be glorified for who He was by what He did. In other words, My Father, God Almighty prepared this, so that I could further establish, in your presence who I really am. Next, Jesus turned His attention to the blind man. He didn't speak to him or lay hands upon him for healing. He spit on the ground, made clay from the spittle, rubbed the spitty clay into the blind man's eyes, and sent him to wash. Had the blind man refused the spitty clay, gone to another water hole, refused to wash, perhaps he would've remained blind. But he followed instructions, and was rewarded with sight. Perhaps, after the compounded pain of the death of Malcolm X, the family exposed again to public shame, scrutiny and loss, in God's infinite wisdom, He can give them much needed sight.

There is the possibility that Dr. Betty Shabazz allowed her tradition and cultural attitudes toward professional psychotherapy to prevent her from seeing the "system" (foster care, psychological testing) as a viable preventative solution for her family. As a single parent, Betty Shabazz might not have viewed the "system" as an option. Had she had time and adequate support system, she would be alive today.[37]

Historically and culturally, Black families in the church community in particular have not sought counseling or therapy as a means of dealing with unresolved family issues. Family members, very often feel compelled to make choices between moving ahead and loyalty to their ethnic group which can in itself be a source of severe identity conflict for family members. This emotional process and fractures also effect and influence the role ethnicity plays in the family.[38]

In light of these barriers and dynamics that prevail in the Black culture, there needs to be a systemic collaborative approach that will permit people to explore and experience on a conscious level the reality of transformational possibilities.

One of the many sustaining qualities in the Black church has been the dimension of Black pastoral care. It has been the pastor and the community at large who provided after the spiritual and emotional needs of their constituents in

---

[37] Boyd-Franklin, Nancy. *Black Families in Therapy.* New York: The Guilford Press, 1989, p. 22.

[38] Monica McGoldrick, John K. Pearce and Joseph Giordano. *Ethnicity and Family Therapy.* New York: The Guilford Press, 1982, p. 91.

family crises.[39] Church leaders are the "first line of defense" for many families against domestic violence, but they seldom are ready for the difficult questions that come up, adds Carl Mangold, an ordained clergyman in The Evangelical Lutheran Church in America. Cornel West makes a brilliant assessment as he relates to the historical and cultural stereotypes rooted in the minds of American society as it concerns the Black culture and its ethnicity. He makes factual presentations regarding the tremendous forces of racism, that's rooted in unhealthy cultural stereotypes that leaves the Black community feeling undefined, unfit and misguided within a biased racial climate.[40] These forces have played an active part in the Black community that fosters abandonment, alienation and isolation, leaving the community void of its dignity to receive the quality of life, necessary to obtain upward mobility. Upward mobility acts as a catalyst necessary to empower any community socially, economically, politically, psychologically, emotionally and spiritually.

It is within this framework that we can learn to respect and appreciate different theoretical value systems in an attempt to utilize various disciplines and methodologies as a tool for social change, justice and social mobility.

In the context of this discussion, what would be the greatest challenge and contribution to offer the African American families? In an attempt to mobilize their resources for surviving crises, how can we provide and obtain upward mobility, in an effort to enhance their quality of life in the presence of dysfunction, traditional and cultural barriers that stifle growth in our families? How can this problem be resolved?

---

[39] Wimberly, Edward P. *Pastoral Care in the Black Church.* Nashville: Abingdon, 1979, p. 35.
[40] West, Cornel. *Race Matters.* New York: Vintage Books, 1993, p. 6.

Betty Shabazz and her family is a classic and tragic example of how much, one African American family's generational recycled pain ignite us all. The swiftness with which the larger Black family galvanized to offer legal support, donate blood, raise money for medical treatment and stand final vigil speaks to what has always been our sublime capacity to sound the drum and heed the call when beloved members of the tribe are in trouble! The painful reality and reminder of what happens when family members keep secrets which are both detrimental and unethical.

It's time we learned that recovering from pain and tragedy takes not just time but also therapeutic interventions. The course of action would be to present an initiative of change, creativity and a paradigm shift that will identify major systemic road blocks that prevent Black families from reaching a level of actualization in order to live life fully and responsibly, in the presence of family dysfunction and tragedy.

Because of this tragedy, I will be devoted to sending a clear message to the Afro-American families. Yes, "The System is an OPTION. Not only is it an option, it is a viable service that is available to families short-lived or prolonged in time of need. It is a service that can provide families with:

- A time to rethink their situation for growth and development at a time of crisis
- A time to heal
- A time to break the cycle of family destructive behavior
- A time to let someone else do what we can no longer do, and perhaps
- To give yourself permission to give up some power and share it with others

Cheryl Sanders offers from her vantage point, that any

one of us can promote social transformation in a sustained, sacrificial manner without a willingness to be changed ourselves. Can we invoke renewed empathy for our own, "in this boat together," so to speak, navigating our way along that inlet called "hope" from lagoon to ocean and back. If we can bring ourselves to profess hope and empathy, and an unselfish desire to empower black people as the "twilight" dawns in America, then certainly we can profess faith in a God "who is able to do exceedingly abundantly above all that we ask or think, according to the power that worketh in us" (Eph. 3:20).[41]

More research is needed in the role that religion and mental health plays in Black families as we enter "uncharted territories."

Ethical Reflections – Racism and Sexism

In what ways does racism and sexism mar and defect African-American relationships between black women and black men?

One of the ethical issues women have been made to believe is their inferiority to white culture and black males. This double victimization is a debilitating racism and sexism that diminishes and undermines the ability of African American women and men to establish mutually satisfying relationships.

Historically, the black community has always depended upon the black church to set the parameters and goals of good and bad, right and wrong, moral and ethics in its constituency. The black community must consider in what

---

[41] Sanders, Cheryl J. Hope and Empathy: "Toward an Ethic of Black Empowerment" *The Journal of Religious Thought* Vol. 52, Number 2, and Vol. 53, Number 1 (1996).

ways, the black church can achieve liberation and reconciliation for their constituents in the thriving environment of racism and sexism.

Toinette M. Eugene describes the unethical ways in which African American relationships have been dehumanized and victimized. "The greatest dehumanization or violence that actually can occur in racist and/or sexist situations happens when persons of the rejected racial – or gender-specific group begin to internalize the judgments made by others and become convinced of their own personal inferiority. Obviously, the most affected and thus dehumanized victims of the experience are Black women. Many incidents have been recorded where the dehumanizational affect has taken such significant effects on the clergy wives, where the damage was so profound, it is almost immeasurable. A pastor was caught in an adulterous relationship so blatant, that it caused an outrage in the church. The pastor had been involved with several women, who came forth at the same time. In his defense, the pastor, indicated his sexual indiscretions were caused by the frigidity of his wife. The distraught wife indicated that it must indeed be her fault, because her husband was a "Man of God." On another occasion, a pastor was brought before a tribunal of bishops on a charge of homosexuality. The presider of the tribunal called the pastor's wife to task, and accused her of being "not woman enough to attract her husband's affections." On another occasion, a pastor's wife appealed to a local council of clergy for their support of her candidacy for election on the school board of education. She was advised that in spite of her energy, education, and qualifications, the council did not feel she was the best electable candidate. She later found out, the council discussed her dark skin complexion, and her overweight presentation, instead of her ability and qualifications. The council decided she had no chance to win against the young white insurance salesman she was running against. The rejection by the clergy group had such a profound effect on the pastor's wife, and the reasons, for the rejection hurt her so deeply, that she withdrew her candidacy from the race altogether. Racism and sexism diminish the ability of black women and men to establish relationships of mutuality, integrity, and trust. Racism and sexism undermine the black communities in which we live, pray, and work out our salvation in the sight of God and one another. However, in coming to terms with racism and sexism as oppressions affecting us all, the black church does have access to the black community in ways that many other institutions do not. The black church has a greater potential to achieve both liberation and reconciliation by attending carefully to the relationships which have been weakened between black males and females.[42] The black church has an unparalleled option to model these gospel values to live an unconditional acceptance. By offering from its storehouse an authentic understanding of black spirituality and sexuality, the black church becomes paradigmatic of the reign of God materializing and entering into our midst.[43]

The author further elaborates that because the black church has access, and is often indeed the presiding and official agent in the process of sexual socialization, it has a potentially unlimited opportunity to restore the ancient covenant of Scripture and tradition which upholds the beauty of black love in its most profound meaning. Wherever black

---

[42] Eugene, Toinette M., *Sexuality and Sources for Theological Reflection,* Ed. James B. Nelson and Sandra P. Longfellow. Louisville, Kentucky: Westminister John Knox Press, 1994, p. 109.
[43] Ibid

love is discouraged or disparaged as an unfashionable or unattainable expression between black women and black men, the black church has an unparalleled option to model these gospel values of love and unconditional acceptance. By offering from its storehouse an authentic understanding of black spirituality and sexuality, the black church becomes paradigmatic of the reign of God materializing and entering into our midst.

Toinette describes ethical implications of black spirituality and sexuality as two of the most serious ethical challenges that the contemporary black church must address. Michelle Wallace agrees that experience of distrust has driven a wedge between black women and black men.

For perhaps the last fifty years there has been a growing distrust, even hatred between black men and black women. It has been nursed along, not only by racism on the part of whites, but by an almost deliberate ignorance on the part of blacks about the sexual politics of their experience in this country. This basic distrust between black women and black men accounts for the inability of the black community to mobilize as it once could and did.

The religious aspect of black sexuality, by which the basic dimension of our self-understanding and way of being in the world as black male and female persons, has been distorted into a form of black sexism.

The black church must re-employ the power of black spirituality as a personal and collective response of black women and black men to the gracious presence of the God who lives and loves within us, calling us to liberating relationships with one another and with all people on Earth.

In the following chapter, I intend to embrace and explore the diversity of spiritual disciplines that play an active part in the life of clergy wives. Many clergy wives have successfully incorporated various spiritual disciplines that have the capacity to facilitate intimacy that fosters a growing and experimental relationship with God.

The discipline of solitude allows the clergy wife to reflect and get in touch with her feelings and permitting her to connect to the foundational self. It will allow her to get underneath the façade and become liberated as she experiences the uniqueness of her own personhood.

CHAPTER FOUR

Spiritual Disciplines that Change Lives

Spiritual Life Issues

Spiritual disciplines are agents of change with creative and growth producing practices that bring people closer to the abundance of God and into the lives of others. Spiritual discipline is a humbling experience that allows individuals to reflect, contemplate, and provoke positive energy to seek God with a greater intensity. It is this type of intensity that maintains balance and continuity in ministry and ones personal life. Richard J. Foster stated:

> The disciplines are God's way of getting us into the ground; they put us where He can work within us and transform us. By themselves the spiritual disciplines can do nothing; they can only get us to the place where something can be done.[44]

As an ordained minister and clergy wife, spiritual disciplines have been a spiritual awakening and a refurbishing

---

[44] Foster, Richard J. *Celebration of Discipline: The Path to Spiritual Growth*. New York: Harper, San Francisco, 1978, p. 7,

of the mind as I strive to develop spiritual life through corporate disciplines. These disciples have the intensity to activate transformational possibilities and psychological wholeness in the lives of others.

In continuing to anticipate the challenges that will impact the clergy wives throughout the country, I look forward to new beginnings, new celebrations, new opportunities and a new paradigm shift. As I embrace the disciplines of meditation, prayer, solitude and slowing down, I begin to hear God speak and hear God's warm acceptance of His will for my life and others. This connection, however, continues to increase as I embrace "change" and transformation within my own life first. This experience affords me another opportunity to embrace prayer designed to create and recreate life changing experiences for the good of clergy wives across the country. In praying the prayer of intercession for clergy families, I find myself listening differently to the heartbeat of God as I near His presence. It is in the context of this energy and presence that I have embraced my worship experience with a daily invoking of listening to God, hearing God and feeling His presence. Worshipping God exposes divine peace and freedom that only spiritual life can bring. Praying allows the individual to share, from the inside out, the most intimate issues. When you pray, you need not ponder the correct grammatical structure of your sentence; you know the God of the universe understands. Prayer can be as long as an all night wrestling match, or as short as two words, "help Lord."

Historically, in the Black church, prayer has always maintained its credibility through its intimate communion with God. Prayer, singing and worshiping experiences have been the stabilizing force and the energy that promotes self-esteem, hope and dignity that our God will deliver us all one day. Clergy wives have been conditioned to mobilize themselves in a prayer vigilance for God to sustain them in their efforts to balance their family life, career and ministry. Prayer has been one of the spiritual disciplines that give hope and meaning in the lives of clergy wives. As a matter of fact, each day in the life of the clergy wife is defined by a series of disciplines mastered to the point of being almost automatic: the discipline of listening, the discipline of discretion, the discipline of singing, the discipline of encouragement, and of course, the discipline of self-survival.

One of the ways spiritual disciplines can play an active part in the lives of clergy wives is to develop and formalize ways to implement these disciplines within the new curriculum design and symposiums. For the past 20 years, I have noticed several organizations I had visited, had a tendency to focus most of their attention on the productivity of their role, their status and living up to the expectations of their husbands and congregations. This futile attempt to uncover who they really are only diminishes the authentic self. In order to develop the authentic self, there needs to be a paradigm shift and a rethinking of how to incorporate various spiritual disciplines into these various organizations that will make a valuable investment into change, growth and transformation. There needs to be a safeguard in place, focusing its attention on personal improvement and mentorship. This methodology would honor the unique needs of clergy wives through support groups that acknowledge strengths and affirm transformational possibilities, in an effort to achieve and master their goals. Introducing and building more spiritual disciplines into the classes and other aspects of various meetings will provide a self-reflective energy for women to harness their need to focus on their role. As Warren Bennie states: "Letting the self emerge is the essential task of leaders."[45]

This author believes that we are presently in a time of restoration for spiritual reestablishment of the destroyed building of humanity. It is a period of returning to God – a journey that the Old Testament prophets Daniel and Ezekiel foretold. Presently, the clergy wife is going through a period of reformation. It is her time, it is her hour for improving and correcting and removing all of the faults as an illuminator of the body of Christ. This reformation, repentance, and restoration for the clergy wife affords her the opportunity to finally hear that original voice of God that called her in the garden. It also comes at a crucial time in the history of the church as we enter the era of the 21st century.

Restoration through Spiritual Disciplines

The discipline of solitude allows the clergy wife to reflect and get in touch with her feelings and permitting her to connect to the foundational self. It will allow her to get underneath the façade and become liberated as she experiences the uniqueness of her own personhood.[46] The discipline of slowing down offers a real challenge to clergy wives since clergy wives are about doing. Slowing down facilitates intimacy that fosters a growing and experiential relationship with God. It is within this context that she experiences a culture change that leads to transformation through liberation. I agree with Nicki Vandergrift who asserts:

Slowing down facilitates intimacy in its many forms and allows for the disengaging from

---

[45] Cashman, Kevin. *Leadership From The Inside Out: Becoming a Leader for Life*. Provo, UT: Executive Excellence Publishing, 1998, p. 120.

[46] Vandergrift, Nicki Verploegen, *Organic Spirituality: A Sixfold Path for Contemplative Living*. New York: Orbis Books, 2000, p. 76.

preoccupations that prevent reflectiveness.[47]

For centuries, African American clergy wives have lived their lives believing the value of church work is found in the consumption of what they do and the quantity of that work. In addition, their theology maintains their belief that "Only what they do for Christ will last" as per the hymn and scripture:

> "Whatsoever ye do in Word or deed, do all in the Name of the Lord Jesus, giving thanks to God and The Father by Him." Col. 3.7[48]

Clergy wives see their role as a catalyst and an agent of change that fulfilling her obligation and obedience to do the will of God through the exercise of "doing." These women have never considered the spiritual disciplines as a productive tool for transformation, since their focus is on productivity. Walter Wink asserts:

> Every dynamic new force for change is under girded by rigorous disciplines. The slack decadence of culture-Christianity cannot produce athletes of the spirit. Those who are the bearers of tomorrow's transformation undergo what others might call disciplines, but not to punish themselves or to ingratiate themselves to God. They simply do what is necessary to stay spiritually alive, just as they eat food and drink water to stay physically alive. One of these disciplines, perhaps the most important discipline of all, is prayer.[49]

---

[47] ibid
[48] _Holy Bible KJV_
[49] Wink, Walter. _The Powers That Be: Theology For A New Millennium._ New York: Galilee Doubleday, 1998, p. 180.

George McClain further addresses the common threads of institutions in their inability to accurately define spirituality.

> We are called to address the inner spirituality of institutions and to confront the evil which besets them with the kind of spiritual care uniquely entrusted to us as Christians. We engage in this confrontation in the confidence that God really does want health and wholeness for institutions as well as for individuals and that God is already at work nudging the church or institution towards greater fidelity to its godly purpose.[50]

Having the opportunity to read *Celebration of Discipline* has been a spiritual awakening and a refurbishing of the mind to develop a balanced spiritual life through these corporate disciplines. It has exposed me to an accelerated transformational journey as I focus my energies on striving for Excellency as I stay attuned to the source of my passion, strength and vision in ministry.

This experience has been an humbling and redemptive journey that allowed me to identify and confront my areas of neglect in these various disciplines. As a result, my reflections and contemplations have provoked a positive energy to seek God with a greater intensity in an effort to maintain balance and continuity in ministry and in my personal life.

As I accept the challenge that will impact my ministry and other ministries throughout the world, I look forward to new beginnings, new celebrations and new opportunities to grow without limits.

---

[50] McClain, George D. *Claiming All Things For God: A Guide To Prayer, Discernment, and Ritual For Social Change.* Nashville, Tennessee: Abingdon Press, 1985, p. 85.

Through this integrated learning process of study and practice, I have developed a greater appreciation for how these disciplines work and have contributed to my personal walk with the Lord. With the increased demands and dilemmas facing ministry today, I can attest to the reality of the peace and the personal freedom I have embraced throughout this entire experience. The disciplines certainly have challenged me beyond my own imagination and expectations.

Richard Foster asserts that in contemporary society our adversary majors in three things: noise, hurry, and crowds. If he can keep us engaged in "much ness" and "many ness," he will rest satisfied. Psychiatrist Carl Jung once remarked, "Hurry is not of the devil, it *is* the devil."

If we hope to move beyond the superficialities of our culture, including our religious culture, we must be willing to go down into the recreating silences, into the inner world of contemplation. In their writings all the masters of meditation beckon us to be pioneers in this frontier of the Spirit. Though it may sound strange to modern ears, we should without shame enroll as apprentices in the school of contemplative prayer.[51]

Celebration of Disciplines has afforded me an opportunity to redefine, redevelop and reposition my focus to include personal goals, personal mastery, personal ministry, family and ministry. I intend to affect change in the lives of others as I continually strive to enter into God's presence for divine direction. I understand that it is my own decision to walk in continual fellowship and humility of heart and in my actions and attitude before God. In an effort to

---

[51] Foster, Richard J. *Celebration of Disciplines: The Path To Spiritual Growth.* New York: Harper San Francisco Publisher, 1978, p. 15.

embrace His perpetual grace and mercy upon my life, I attempt to listen and hear God as I contemplate and embrace the next millennium.

People who understand the importance of personal development and who have cultivated a high degree of self-mastery are the ones most able to sail through challenging times with confident balance. They've learned to deeply listen and respond skillfully to the subtle whispers that warn them when they are drifting out of balance. As a result, they are more likely to eat when they are hungry and to rest and renew themselves when they are tired. By recognizing and reducing the harmful accumulations of stress, they are able to live in a more balanced and more disease-resistant way. In the process of developing the mindfulness necessary to recognize the master stress, we can also deepen our mind-body-spirit connection as a whole. This allows us to gain the inner strength and understanding necessary to meet every situation in a more balanced, centered way.[52]

To address a new paradigm shift for clergy wives at their various meetings will be both challenging and creative. The spiritual disciplines of solitude and slowing down can first be introduced and integrated in the context of the classroom setting. Each facilitator will introduce the two new spiritual disciplines designed to offer self-reflection in an attempt to improve oneself spiritually for the purpose of transformational possibilities. This exercise will take place in the beginning of each session. At the conclusion, a discussion focusing on the responses and reactions to the spiritual disciplines will provide an opportunity to determine its success.

---

[52] Joel Levey and Michelle Levey. *Living In Balance: A Dynamic Approach For Creating Harmony and Wholeness in a Chaotic World*, Berkeley, CA: Conari Press, 1998, p. 284-285.

Every service, every seminar, every class, and every exercise presented and performed in annual conferences is done in the hopes of presenting a transformational process of improvement for the success of their meetings.

In the life of the African American church community, the biblical text has always been the primary source of their communication and relationship with God. I will identify the paradigm shift taken place in the New Interpreter's Bible Commentary that gives relevance of changing the Euro-centric view to an Afro-centric view. This particular view lends itself to a new commentary that relates perceptively the inherited scripture to the unfolding present.

I have developed a further understanding of Proverbs 31:10-31, by examining the ancient Eastern Literature and culture as it pertains to the realistic presentation of the entire text.

Black women are so often called upon to appear strong, independent and self-confident. Church is the one place we feel safe enough to wear our vulnerability on the sleeves of our designer dresses. We feel secure in stitching our neediness into the hems of our softly tailored suits. When we share our tears and fears with our male ministers, we forge one of the most intimate relationships possible between two human beings.

CHAPTER FIVE

A Biblical Text that Authenticates and Transforms Lives

One of the critical areas of biblical concern, in many of our churches, involves the interpretation of Proverbs 31:10-31(NASB)[53]. Traditionally, there are scholars that have interpreted this scripture, so as to suggest that women intending to be virtuous must live up to the standard of this scripture. In the African American church, it has been every woman's conviction that her life is to be spent offering herself to this effort. Women are taught that this high expectation is a mandate from God for Christian living. After reviewing the introduction to the New Interpreter's Bible Commentary, I was relieved by the essential and critical changes made in the last four decades. The author, Leander E. Keck acknowledges the obvious and apparent stagnation of various denominations, the exegetical approach as "text-centered." That is, the commentators focus primarily on the text in its final form rather than on (a) a meticulous rehearsal of problems of scholarship associated with a text, (b) a thorough reconstruction of the pre-history of the text, or (c) an exhaustive rehearsal of the text's interpretive history.

---

[53] *Holy Bible, NASB*

These additional changes will affect Christians of all persuasions and ecclesial identities generally accorded the Bible normative status in matters of faith and ethics, and so looked to it for the answers to life's problems; by the nineties, however, many have concluded that the Bible's pervasive patriarchalism makes it the source more of the problem than of the solution. The New Interpreter's Bible on the other hand, enlists the participation of a significant number of women and minority scholars. One of these shifts have changed the Euro-centric view to an Afro-centric view that lends itself to a new commentary that relates perceptively the inherited scripture to the unfolding present. In addition to the recent work done, biblical study has undergone important shifts.[54]

Ellen Davis, reports in her commentary that,

> The passage shows that wife and husband functioning as a team, the two faces of the family. The wife more private and the husband more public.[55]

It is essential to underscore this inequitable distribution of gender importance. This type of imbalance is definitely not a team effort but rather portrays power and control. The patriarchal hierarchical system of the church has convinced women to pursue this virtuous role model, as scriptural, revelant, and contemporary. Proverbs 31, further perpetuates an unrealistic life style for clergy wives to adhere to, thus creating spousal abuse: physically, mentally, emotionally, and spiritually.

---

[54] Keck, Leander E., " Introduction" *The New Interpreter's Bible*, Nashville, TN: Abingdon Press, 1994, p. 2-3.
[55] Davis, Ellen F. *Proverbs, Ecclesiastes, and the Song of Songs*, Louisville, Kentucky: Westminster John Knox Press, 2002, p. 154.

In verse 23, we read, "The husband is known in the gates, when he sitteth among the Elders of the Land." The husband exercises his authority in public, but her life is confined to the home where she performs domestic and managerial duties because this is her reality and this is what is expected. Women today pursue this unrealistic lifestyle, because so-called biblical authoritarians have passed on wrong information and judgement without properly interpreting Proverbs 31, of ancient Israel, as a principle not to be adhered to in this 21st century society.

Coming from a different perspective, this passage about the virtuous women can be helpful for women today. Ellen Davis presents a wonderful tribute to this virtuous woman. She claims that, although the topic of good and bad women is common in Egyptian and Babylonian wisdom literature, nothing in all ancient near Eastern literature matches this tribute to a woman's strength, dignity, and social power.

Bell Hooks expressed in her book, "Teaching to Transgress,"[56] a great concern for the ability of women to step beyond the systemic boundaries of our society. She expressed the need for women to blot out traditional lines of control in order to create a new atmosphere of liberation through theory and practice. Her liberation reminds me of Proverbs 31: 13-19, when the virtuous woman was seen for the very first time as a positive role model, resourceful and liberating. Bell Hooks further elaborates her own process, one that permits people to explore and experience, on a conscious level, the reality of feminist transformational possibilities. It is within this framework that we learn to respect and appreciate her theoretical value system, as it pertains to her main thrusts, which is to abolish the traditional

---

[56] Hooks, Bell. *Teaching to Transgress: Education as the Practice of Freedom*, New York: Routledge, 1994, p. 70.

bias and sexist prejudices in the society, the educational system, and in the classroom. Teaching to transgress is at the heart of freedom and justice in the classroom. It is the dignity of one woman, who developed an infectious attitude towards rethinking the traditional and conventional style of learning in the classroom.

Proverbs 31:10-31, is an acrostic poem that reveals the portrait of matriarchal wisdom. This proverb is not to be taken literally, nor does it suggest that Christian women must subject themselves to an unbelievable blueprint for their daily lives.

This poem should be viewed as ancient Near Eastern literature and culture. Revisiting this scripture reminds me of the tremendous demands and expectations, that people and systems have placed on the role of the clergy wife. Ellen Davis exegetes Proverbs 31 by suggesting:

> "The present poem was probably created, not to honor one particularly praiseworthy woman, but rather to underscore the central significance of women's skilled work in a household-based economy."[57]

In vs (13-19), this woman is seen as a manufacturer, importer, manager, realtor, farmer, seamstress, upholster and merchant. On the flip side, we find a resourceful woman, living against the odds, born out of her time and living outside of the box. Pleasing herself, pleasing her God, her children, and her husband. Here, she is seen as a positive role model. A woman of strong character, great wisdom, exemplary of managerial skills and compassion. She is a highly effective

---

[57] Davis, Ellen. *Proverbs, Ecclesiastes, and the Song of Songs.* Louisville, Kentucky: Westminster John Knox Press, 2002, p. 154.

woman, operating in her field of interest. In these few verses, her authentic self expresses her creating values which sets her apart from other women who have been conditioned to accept their reality, without asking challenging questions and waiting for answers. I believe it was both her amazing virtue and maternal wisdom that allowed her voice to be heard. She demonstrates her ability to express herself, and influence others, through her style, grace, and wisdom.

The Gender Question

How does the Bible address women taking a leadership role in a patriarchal society in the 21st century? What happens when God sets a higher precedence on ability and availability opposed to gender and tradition?

In Judges, Chapter four, Deborah offers a brilliant presentation in leading Israel as judge and prophetess, as she leads Israel into safety. As a result of her courageous initiative, Barak backed down from his power since Deborah was recognized as one who hears from God.

> Barak said to her, "If you go with me, I will go; but if you don't go with me, I won't go. "Very well," Deborah said, "I will go with you. But because of the way you're going about this, the honor will not be yours for the Lord will hand Sisera over to a woman so Deborah went with Barak to Kedesh. (NASB Judges 4:8-9)[58]

Deborah accepted the challenge to take the lead, as an agent of change to defeat King Jabin and to lure Sisera, the commander of Jabin's army into the hand of Barak. After

---

[58] *Holy Bible, NASB*

20 years of oppression at the hands of the Canaanites, Barak perhaps lacked the faith in God, that he knew Deborah had to lead the people into safety.

What happens when there is a lack of male leaders stepping forward at a critical time of history when decisions need to be made and actions need to be enforced?

Unlike many of the other heroes in this book, Deborah was "judge": one to whom people came for judgment (4:4-5). She was a real judge for judgment; and it is interesting from the point of view of social history that this first named judicial officer in the Bible should have been a woman, and a married woman at that. Two of her other "vital statistics" have caused rather more comment. What is it about her that leads to her being termed a "prophetess."

Judges 4 is very much a story in which women take the lead; and this is the more striking, because it is an episode from national life, not a more domestic narrative like the Book of Ruth. It is Deborah, the widely acknowledged judge, who issues a summons to Barak. When he appears before her, she gives him instructions in the name of God. When he responds cautiously, like Gideon, she agrees to accompany him – but with a warning that the praises to be sung will not be his, but a woman's.[59]

Although Deborah accepted the challenge to lead the children of Israel to safety, Barak was the one that received honor in the New Testament, in the Epistle of Hebrews as

[59] Auld, Graeme A. *The Daily Study Bible Series*: Louisville, Kentucky: Westminster John Knox Press, 1984, p. 152-153.

one of the heroes of faith when Deborah was the champion of faith in the book of Judges.

In contrast, to the 21st century, the patriarchal dominance in the African American church continues to prevail in its efforts to neutralize and restrict women from preaching in the pulpit and from being ordained. Yet it is the patriarchal leadership that promotes the female population to raise the most money, evangelize the community for church growth and maintain the standard of holiness and morality while the male population are exempt from exercising morality and fidelity practices.

Male dominance in African American churches was expressed most clearly by the fact that Black women were forbidden to be ordained and to preach from a pulpit. These prohibitions continue to be "justified" by reference to biblical sources. At a Black Methodist preachers meeting of the Washington annual conference in 1890, the question was posed: "Is woman inferior to man?" The chairman of the meeting replied: "Sad as it may be, woman is an inferior to man as man is to God."

Keeping Black women out of the pulpit of certain churches constitutes what Michael Eric Dyson calls ecclesiastical apartheid, and is surely connected to the reality that preaching, as Gilkes puts it, "is the most masculine aspect of black religious ritual. In spite of the progress of women in ministry, preaching remains overwhelmingly a form of male discourse." There may also be a deep psychological resistance to the very idea that a group of men (even though they will be in the numerical minority in most Black churches) should have to sit and listen to a woman (preacher) telling them what to do and what not to do.

Subtle and not so subtle notions that Black women, like

children, are best seen and not heard, and that a Black woman should stand several paces behind her man permeated religious circles, and were also present in prescriptions for proper behavior by Black women in civil society.

How does scripture address women as it pertains to their rights? How does God address His relationship with women in reference to their gifts, skills, worship and their relationship to God?

Bishop McKenzie speaks of the double standard principle outside the realm of sexual behavior. Women in ministry are under constant pressure to explain and defend their call to the ministry, and their success or failure affects the women clergy who follow them.

One of the most blatant manifestations of male privilege in Black churches occurs within, to use Marcia Dyson's language, preachers prey on women parishioners for sexual favors. Such behavior is certainly not restricted to Black preachers. It occurs in white churches, the White House, and other places of worship outside the Christian tradition. Some men of the cloth consider such sexual exploits their right. This point is worth considering with respect to Dr. Martin Luther King, Jr. – one of the world's greatest champions for civil and human rights. Dyson insinuates Dr. King's behavior within the rampant patriarchy of the Black church.

Black women are so often called upon to appear strong, independent and self-confident. Church is the one place we feel safe enough to wear our vulnerability on the sleeves of our designer dresses. We feel secure in stitching our neediness into the hems of our softly tailored suits. When we share our tears and fears with our male ministers, we forge one of the most intimate relationships possible between two human beings. If we're the least bit careless about our principles and prayers, it becomes easy to confuse spiritual and emotional needs with erotic desires and to act on them inappropriately.[60]

What is the future and new directions for the Black church? What are the ongoing challenges to the overwhelming, persistence and agonizing patriarchal attitudes that prevent women's liberation and solidarity to exist?

Historically, the patriarchal leadership has formed a subtle alliance to manipulate biblical text to suggest and confine African American women to a lesser and limited role in the church, for the sole purpose of protecting the Black male identity. In an unusual appeal to Black male ministers, James Cone urges them to take the issue of women's liberation seriously and understand the depth of sexism in Black churches as well as the connection between racism and sexism; learn how to really listen to women's stories of pain and struggle; and support women's leadership roles in the church, including that of minister. He boldly advocates affirmative action strategies for Black women in churches so that they will be represented equally in all positions of responsibility. And finally, he calls for serious discussion of the role of Black women in the church and asserts passionately that "The black church cannot regain its Christian integrity unless it is willing to face head-on the evil of patriarchy and seek to eliminate it."

Many people in the Church, including church-school teachers and pastors, tend to pick and choose biblical texts that suit their own tastes and personal values, without making

---

[60] Johnnette Betsch Cole and Beverly Guy-Shaftall. *Gender Talk: The Struggle for Women's Equality in African American Communities*, New York: One World Ballentine Books, 2003, p. 109-117.

much attempt to reflect critically on how these values often only mirror their own narrow socialization. Furthermore, Church leaders barely study the ancient historical and cultural background that gave rise to this Word of God. What is forgotten is that the Bible confronts us with a series of theologically motivated histories of ancient communities (including families and households) in crisis or struggle, trying to make sense out of constantly changing socioeconomic and political circumstances.[61]

In the formation of my Christian experience, I have witnessed in the 20th through the 21st centuries, a grave disparity in the interpretation of the biblical text that men were the only gender to preach the gospel.

Afro-American women from my Christian experience understood that they were not allowed to preach because of their gender. Their world was limited to the missionary society. In this society, they exercised and expressed their gifts through worship. They exercised their teaching and leadership abilities with satisfaction and without challenge.

In contrast, I have witnessed this same patriarchal leadership sending women missionaries to foreign countries to start ministries. They provided oversight although they were not called pastors, yet they were pastoring until the church grew to a comfortable size. At this time, a male pastor would be assigned to relieve the missionary of her duties. She returned to her local church feeling displaced, fragmented and disfranchised. She was exposed to a male role, male authority and pastoral responsibilities. But she was not allowed to fulfill, complete and authenticate the purpose of her mission. With this type of exposure, she was unable to celebrate her achievement of finding herself in a

---

[61] Felder, Cain Hope Felder. *Troubling Biblical Waters: Race, Class, and Family.* Maryknoll, New York: Orbis Books, 1989, p. 154.

conflicting place with God and with man. If she did celebrate herself, God would punish her, scripture would condemn her and her sisters would be angry with her for stepping out of the traditional box and into the box of revelatory knowledge. This mode of transition cannot be understood in a patriarchal dominate environment that refuses to share the power among gifted women.

The misinterpretation of scripture and the need to control and dominate women from exercising their God-given talent is only another way to keep women oppressed, confined, comfortable and complacent.

Biblical text brings meaning to ones Christian experience and transformational wholeness into one's life. As an Afro-American woman in leadership, it is my responsibility to present the gospel in precept and example, in reinforcing scripture that "God is no respecter of persons." (Acts 10:34). KJV[62]. By claiming the freedom of God, Afro-American clergy wives can open themselves to new possibilities for human existence. The radical freedom of God allows Afro-American clergy women to completely orient their existence.[63] Afro-American women no longer need the approval of their European counterparts. Their belief in God is enough to sustain them as they pursue their roles as representatives of God in their communities. It is my passion and position as an Afro-American leader, in my community to strive to present God as our sustainer, provider and our everlasting Prince of Peace.

As I embrace this 21st century, my vision, my energies, and my focus will address the forces that impact and stifle the daily lives of the Afro-American community. These paralyzing forces of racism, class distinction, and gender

---

[62] _Holy Bible, KJV_
[63] Evans, James H. Jr. _We Have Been Believers._ Minneapolis: Fortress Press, 1992, p. 68.

discrimination creates the loss of hope, absence of meaning, and social frustration. As a professional Black marriage and family therapist and ordained minister, I am faced with an enormous bias from "old school" authority in the church that segregates women in the body of Christ by the use of misinterpretation and manipulation of scripture. I plan to take an active role, to insure that other women have the opportunity to express their views, and to be acknowledged as the leaders they were always meant to be.

A redesigned curriculum must reflect change. It must be focused, targeted, thoughtful and goal-oriented. It must confront the membership spiritually, cognitively; effectively and behaviorally. It must be both didactic and practical, embracing the concepts of enabling and empowerment through the sharing of fresh resources, including publications, websites, and even the development of "hotlines" which can be staffed by involved, willing women, offering support and mentorship.

CHAPTER SIX

A Curriculum Design that Nurtures, Cultivates, and Empowers Lives

Many organizations choose the path of least resistance, by cultivating curriculums that are neutral to denominational issues, and palatable to organizational tastes. In so doing, they establish acceptance by all, thus maintaining their positions, status, and power. This is called, "going along, to get along." Neutrality then becomes a force that prevents new, fresh, creative minds from influencing and establishing vision and enlightenment for today's challenges. Regardless of the longevity of those who sit in the seats of authority, if their terms of office do not produce help for the sisterhood, then their tenure has been in vain. Through a curriculum design, the use of the best trained staff available and making use of the most appropriate scholarly literature, films, and facilities, can begin to expose voids, expand horizons, and experience change in their sisterhood.

It is important to understand the lesson of history. If history is not understood, and/or properly interpreted, it will repeat itself. Whatever has happened will happen: nothing different, nothing new. Repetition has a tendency to become patternistic, and a pattern in and of itself, is safe, but it is determinable and predictable. When you are able to determine results and predict outcome, your product is usually bland and somewhat tasteless. With the development of the Internet, automation and modern day technology, the pursuit of excellence is almost without limit. The tools that are available for record keeping, advertising and teaching, can enhance almost every arena of learning. Meeting planners and developers can be equipped with information to change their results and turn their advertising around. Yet none of these updated mechanism will impose themselves on anyone. You can maintain the status quo, if you feel it is your responsibility to do so. The same thing applies to thinking: new ideas, new disciplines and new training has to be applied, to address the issues and present them at various meetings. Usually, the classes presented were always role related to fit the various roles of the minister's wife. Workshops on how to be a better "first lady", how to be a better "minister's wife", how to be a better "mother of pastor's kids", how to be a better "pastor's home keeper", how to "keep a perpetual smile on your face", but there was nothing designed for the woman, such as how to "better yourself just for you." The presentations for improvement were so single dimensional, they suggest there was no room in the life of the minister's wife for her to consider being or doing anything else.

Change Becomes the Order of the Day

I have noticed in my travels, that change was not drastic, but it was obvious. Themes began to focus on issues of current events. Seminars were being offered in the areas of political science, voter registration prep, family planning, counseling skills, budgeting and planning, etc. These classes opened horizons for vision potential. It said to the woman, "There is a world outside the walls of your church that can use your informed involvement." The history of the clergy wives will attest to the fact that the leadership of this era prepared the women to interact with the community and vicinity where they are located. The clergy wife would not leave her annual conference feeling empowered to become involved in areas where her personality and intelligence could be used to support or influence a cause that was not solely a church related issue, but could perhaps help the sphere of influence of the church. For instance, she could run for a position on the school PTA or Board of Education. She could serve on any number of community boards, and in so doing, represent her church, her husband and herself. Classes in counseling, economics, sociology, psychology, philosophy, journalism, etc, were not being offered. Classes to challenge and influence the total woman, so that in her preparation and development, she could broaden her horizons in scope, vision and potential.

I will introduce a new curriculum design, which addresses the essential components necessary to begin the transformative process. Part of the new curriculum design will include:

1. Family life education
2. The dynamics of marriage and the marital relationship
3. The dynamics of personality

Practical Methodology Issues

Introducing a curriculum design to the clergy wives is critically important to the realization of the vision and its long-term values, and its effect on the lives of clergywomen across the country. Empowering and exposing clergy wives to a new progressive programming, will lead to growth and development.

Donald P. Smith shares how empowering responds to the deep needs of people with God's resources. He shares how when we seek to empower people, they begin to discover channels that link the power of salvation to individuals need for wholeness, hope and meaning for living.[64]

A redesigned curriculum must reflect change. It must be focused, targeted, thoughtful and goal-oriented. It must confront the membership spiritually, cognitively; effectively and behaviorally. It must be both didactic and practical, embracing the concepts of enabling and empowerment through the sharing of fresh resources, including publications, websites, and even the development of "hotlines" which can be staffed by involved, willing women, offering support and mentorship.

The content of the new syllabus can be arranged around the interpersonal needs of women, focusing on three major topics: Family Life Education, including those skills needed in preparation for courtship, marriage and sustained family living; The dynamics of marriage, and the marital relationship including interactions, communication patterns, role expectations and subtle inequalities in marriages which can result in marital distress; and The dynamics of personality, which highlight personality make-up, needs and other factors that foster or impede development and impact the quality of interpersonal relationships.

Central to this newly designed Teaching Series will be strategies for enhancing intimacy, improving negotiation skills within marriage and creative conflict resolution. Participants will also be given knowledge about defining and recognizing

---

[64] Smith, Donald P. *Empowering Ministry: Ways to Grow In Effectiveness.* Louisville, Kentucky: Westminster John Knox Press, 1996, p. 11.

abuse, assertiveness training, marriage enrichment, the concept of mutual submission, and the essential notion of taking responsibility for one's own actions and their consequences.

Course content can be presented in a curriculum within a 12–15 weeks program. There can be two-hour teaching classes to include a certificate or diploma presented by the organization on completion at a graduation ceremony.

This formal process of study will enable and support the learner, encouraging her to make the course content knowledge her own, and give sanction to the learning.

Counseling Methodology and the Process for Implementation

A growth curriculum that promotes change rest heavily upon change agents, i.e., clinical staff, who implements the "growth" design in group and individual settings. These Agents of Change serve as mentors, coaches, counselors and workshop leaders, providing motivation, guidance, and impetus for participant transformation.

Goodrich offers her insight regarding the empowering effects of change when working with women in groups.

When our ministry concentrates on empowerment, our service to God inspires wholeness in lives of God's suffering people, who we also serve. We are empowered by God to empower those whose lives we touch. When that transforms our calling, we see Bible, theology, preaching, worship, and program with new eyes. No longer are they skill-filled tasks of ministry. They become channels by which the power of the Holy Spirit touches the human condition of particular people who have particular needs.[65]

Counseling, a dynamic and constantly evolving discipline, can take place in group or individual settings. The redesign curriculum will utilize both strategies through seminar and mentorship opportunities.

The group setting provides unique features that are lacking in individual counseling. Group participants often experience a sense of "togetherness" by observing that others are struggling with the same problems. This identification with others reduce feelings of isolation and of being alone, supporting a stronger sense of self. The group experience also helps to develop adaptive social skills that are more difficult to impart individually. It is conceived that the workshops or "growth groups" will be structured in design and focused around specific themes.

They can be limited to ten participants each. Possible themes may be assertiveness training; enhancing communication skills and decision making; handling anger; coping with fear, divorce and abandonment issues; fostering a more positive identity; and taking more responsibility for one's needs. Sessions can be one to two hours. Counseling is not a discipline that can be easily mastered; especially in a week of classroom settings and seminars. But the encouraging thing that comes out of these classes is two-fold. One, exposure to the various classes encourages people involved in the various problems being focused upon, to be encouraged by the fact, they are not the only ones going through the situation, and they pick up information to help them better cope with their individual predicament. And two, many students leave the classes determined to pursue

---

[65] Smith, Donald P. *Empowering Ministry: Ways to Grow in Effectiveness.* Louisville, Kentucky : Westminster John Knox Press, 1996, p.10.

educational goals, to become counselors themselves, regardless of the time and effort required. They are inspired to the point of determination.

There is also a need for sound, therapeutic techniques in individual counseling, mentorship and follow-up to the group process in order to effect change. Central to this process will be active listening and logical discussion, allowing the participant to be heard and understood, and permitting her to appraise reality, see alternatives and anticipate consequences. Closely connected to this process is participant sharing or ventilation, which can release energy which then becomes available for us in achieving more effective social functioning.

Other techniques used to spur growth might include role-playing, which breaks through resistances, allowing participants to test out new skills and promotes spontaneity and emotional action. This powerful teaching device is useful in both individual and group settings. Coaching, that is, urging the participant toward action and self-expression is important and can be a profound therapeutic tool. Through coaching, the leader uses professional knowledge, experience and authority to help the participant move forward, equipped with a strategy for decision-making and constructive action.

All of these strategies, whether in group or individual sessions, will be employed to enable the participant to grow, to acquire self-understanding, to anticipate and control disabling responses to her current and predictable future life situations.

Basic to an effective program would require sensitivity and the challenge to address and embrace race, class and gender issues which are basic forces that impact our every day lives. Every fiber of the African American community is impacted by the loss of hope and absence of meaning and social frustration. In an effort to meet the needs of its constituency, Afro-American clergy women in leadership must change in an effort to work towards promoting healthy personality development and satisfactory social functioning as it relates to the multiplicity of various family members, both individually and collectively.

My concerns in ministry are based on actualizing individuals where they are by providing them with an opportunity to discuss the fundamental crises in Black America, as it relates to race, class and gender issues. These forces affect the problem of Black poverty, the breakdown of family, spiritual impoverishment, and the denial of class division and gender inequality. It is these concerns that "fit" in the framework of my ministry as a means of reaching out through the intervention of workshops, seminars and a collaborative effort through a forum of care providers, psychologist, social workers, marriage and family therapist and clergy. This forum would be designed to address issues relating to the development of gender and class diversity. This therapeutic process would include a representation of professionals to form a Christian coalition to assess all possibilities around the forces of race, gender and class issues in Black America. Historically, the church has always been the catalyst in the Black community that addresses those paralyzing forces, in order to bring hope, faith and social mobility in the Black community.

In order to discuss the Christian faith and salvation in the Black community, one must consider the church as the critical force and the most viable energy in the life and survival of Black people in this country. Robert Staples says that it has been a buffer institution which provided many Blacks with an outlet for their frustration in a society which penalized them for their racial membership.[66] My continuation in higher education remains a vital tool and an asset throughout my personal growth and development. The further I excel in this forum; I can assist my constituency by providing a vehicle of social change that will enhance the quality of life, promoting health personality development and satisfactory social functioning within the church and family community. I plan to bring together other Afro-American women in leadership to dialogue and to be active voices for social change. I realize that both Afro-American women and Afro-American men need to work together to affect social change. As a professional Afro-American woman in leadership, I plan to be that uniting force. In my ministry, there will be an opportunity for men and women to come together and change the climate of hopelessness in our community.

As I embrace this 21st century, my vision, my energies and focus will always address the basic forces that impact and stifle the daily lives of the African American community. These paralyzing forces of race, class and gender discrimination impacts the loss of hope, absence of meaning and social frustration. As a professional Black marriage and family therapist and ordained minister, I am faced with an enormous deprivation from clinicians that lack the sensitivity within the scope of the Black church due to their existence of racial discrimination within the mental health profession. In the Black church, the pastor is the "power symbol" and minister that is usually a central figure in the life of the family members. He becomes the catalyst and vehicle that family members reach out for in time of trouble, pain or lose.

There is a large majority of dissident "White" therapists who engage in ignoring religious issues with Black families.

---

[66] Staples, Robert. *Black Masculinity: The Black Males' Role in American Society.* San Francisco, CA: Black Scholar Press, 1982, p. 63

Very often, Black families frame issues in religious terms. The therapist immediately interprets this as a "pathology" within the Black family. As a result, a value conflict can sometimes erupt in which the family ends up disengaging from treatment. The involvement of the minister can take many different forms. They might simply be asked for information and asked for their help in encouraging the family to seek and follow through on treatment. The notion is just as counterproductive as the view that depreciates the importance of racial factors.[67] Christian counseling comes alive in the Black community when qualified therapists are sensitive to ethnic, gender and environmental issues.

My greatest challenge is to affect change within the structure of the mental health profession as I continue to connect and collaborate with the presence of "White" racism. Afro-American clergy women have been leaders in their community, their voice has been silent but the climate is changing. As an Afro-American woman in leadership, I plan to take an active role to insure that other women have the opportunity to speak forth their views and to be acknowledged as the leaders they have always been.

As I begin to address power and justice in the next chapter, I plan to focus my attention on the frustration, degradation, and the patriarchal dominance that clergy wives have had to suffer for centuries. I will also elaborate how every fiber of the African American Community is impacted by the loss of hope and absence of meaning and social frustration.

---

[67] Boyd-Franklin, Nancy. *Black Families in Therapy*. New York: The Guilford Press, 1989, p. 98.

Women have always had the capacity to gel with other women who were ready to share beyond surface generalities and safe genre. In my teaching experience, my joy was to set the climate and parameters of openness, fidelity and solidarity in an attempt to develop a context of empowering and liberating clergy wives to move forward. Moving forward is a participatory process that enables women to see themselves doing what they never imagined would evolve for them.

CHAPTER SEVEN

Closing Argument – Theological Reflections

Historically and theologically, African American clergy wives have maintained a subservient role and the need to intentionally avoid acting on their own needs, impulses and aspirations. In the presence of this political and patriarchial apartheid, women have not had the luxury of participating in the boardroom as it pertains to the global and essential needs of women. The patriarchial systems can not conceivably understand the intrapsychic, emotional and mental needs of women in light of these political intrusions, gender differences, and their patriarchal forces that are designed to disembody, fragment and neutralize women from exercising their creativity, spiritual and intellectual abilities.

In the past 10 years, my social location and theological revolt comes from Black male dominance and oppression from my former church organization experience of 40 years. My struggles became a reality when some oppressed women became my oppressor. This reality came as a result of my husband's decision to leave the organization based on unbiblical rigid rules placed on women that are theologically unsound. These are women who blamed me for forcing my husband to leave the organization so I could preach. The idea, of course, came from their husbands. The patriarchal system has perpetrated a theological belief system of rigid rules that unilaterally controls, dominates and manipulates women, emotionally, mentally and psychologically. In many organizations, and affiliations women are indoctrinated to believe they could not preach, could not vote and could not exercise their gifts, skills and talents on the same level as men. This type of sexist ideas and practices in the church has reduced the gospel to a sidebar discussion and has increased the inhumane captivity of women for the purpose of power and control. In an effort to keep the peace and fire burning at home, they saw me as their enemy. Women unconsciously resented my freedom and liberation. Perhaps, their own oppression, being deprived of their own subjectivity puts any abused woman in a self-hate dilemma. When abused women are oppressed, the signals from their abusers validate that they are nothing without their men and nothing without his validation. This leaves her in a holding position, unable to control her destiny. Instead, she relinquishes her control leaving her husband and abuser the executor of her mindset and her false reality of life.

For centuries, African American women have responded to their matriarchal role in the home and in the church. Their innate capacity to nurture and cultivate their families and contribute to the functionality of their church community has sustained their African American society through their faith in God. In the 21st century, African American women are now much more in touch with their place in a racist and sexist society. They are no longer limited to serve within the context of their home and church community. What are the fears and limitations that block empowerment transformational possibilities?

When women's intrapsychic experiences are blocked by fears, self-criticism and self-blame, they fall into a conforming and noncommittal state of mind leaving them void of transformational possibilities. How can women continue to strive and survive without a voice without an audience and without a community that addresses her needs and pain?

How does the church foster this belief system, and how can the church begin to address these abusive forces and begin to empower and transform lives? The church should be a guide to transformation for all its constituency. In addition, the church should strengthen this transformation process by addressing and exposing relevant social ills throughout the church community by presenting workshops, conferences and symposiums in an effort to minimize malpractices and causes of abuse. Since the church claims to be an institution of love, hope, security and change, however, its' virtues are based on dogma rather than reality. The church should be the place where the most desperate individual is able to come to escape the ravaging pitfalls of sin, degradation and helplessness in the world. The church should be a place of safety, honesty, wholeness and love. But, if for any reason, this wonderful place of refuge has a dark side or double standard, it is created by the men in the church. The men in the church are protected and indulged and the women are violated and abused. This imbalanced attitude changes the church without recourse and resolve into an agent of deformation, degradation and shame.

How is this agent of deformation, degradation and shame played out? Who are the chief players? Women were reduced to voiceless instruments of servitude and pleasure. This was done by the misdirected interpretation of scripture which allowed the men to conduct themselves shamelessly and without any retribution for conduct and behavior, unbecoming the offices they held. The women who were not allowed a "voice" were also robbed of justice. Before America attacked Afghanistan, a film was circulated through the news media showing a woman being beaten mercilessly in the streets by the Taliban for allowing her face guard to accidentally fall from her face. America cringed at the shameless way this woman was beaten down, crying for help and her cries were unheeded. Yet, in the same way, the African American clergy wives have been treated just as shamelessly: howbeit, much more subtle and secretive, nevertheless the abuse was directed with the same viciousness from male to female, from husband to wife, from man of God to woman of God and this too, in the name of religion. The engine for this behavior is fueled primarily by the example of predecessor's behavior: everyone knows it's been done before and believes it will be done again. No man believes that his behavior or conduct is either wrong or unique. It is the way things have been done in society to keep the woman in line. When the slave master humiliated the male slave and indulged himself with the slave wife, the only expression of manliness the male slave had was to take his frustration out on his already abused wife, exposing her to double victimization. This does not justify wife beating but it does set a precedent of its origin. The African American woman has always had to be strong and fight for the semblance of family to exist in our society. When the man of God takes on the responsibility of his role, he often indulges himself with self-appointed awards for which he believes he is entitled. If this reward happens to be an extra marital affair, it is no more demeaning than another suit added to the wardrobe or a newer car sitting in the driveway or an expensive watch strapped to his arm. It is a perk of the job. It is a benefit of the job, it is to be expected, and it is to be understood. The only one that seems to be unruffled by this tolerance is the wife who is expected to stay at home, fix his food, attend his children, clean his house and be a good wife.

My theological perspective has been influenced by Cheryl Townsend Gilkes, who rises up against male attempts to exclude, ignore, trivialize, or marginalize women in a number of capacities[68], she states, "If it wasn't for the women, you wouldn't have a church!" In my practice as a Marriage and Family Therapist for twenty-one (21) years, I have, on more than one occasion, wondered if the curse placed on Eve for her influencing Adam in the Garden of Eden, has now taken on new dimensions. The advent of female misuse and abuse is taken to abhorrent dimensions around the world. There are places in Africa where the clitoris is ritualistically removed from helpless young teenage girls, thus depriving them of the possibility of any sexual pleasure for the rest of their life. In North Africa, Morocco, to be specific, it is an everyday occurrence to see a man riding on his donkey, and struggling along behind him is a withered little woman with a large bundle on her head, trying to keep up, so as not to cause delay, relegated to daily servitude and the sexual pleasure comfort for the man to whom she belongs. Women all over the world are victimized by being savagely beaten, then forced to lay with the same man who beat her and bring him sexual pleasure, get up and fix his food, keep his habitation clean and bare him children; all without recourse. Is this an expansion of the curse? I don't think that would be fair. Nor do I believe this is what God intended for the women. The pain and suffering in childbirth is sufficient enough

---

[68] Gilkes, Cheryl Townsend. *If It Wasn't for the Women: Black women's Experience and Womanist Culture in Church and Community.* Maryknoll, New York: Orbis Books, 2001, p. 98.

punishment for her involvement.. But the plight of the woman reaches into almost every arena of life. What were the intentions of the founding fathers when they wrote, "We hold these truths to be self evident, that all men are created equal." Now we know that "all men" did not include the slave men, but did it also exclude all women, including White women as well. Why did women have to fight so hard during "Women Suffrage" just to get the right and privilege to vote? Were they considered to be too ignorant, too unsophisticated, or just too busy doing household chores to take time out to vote? But still, all of the examples cited above, pole in comparison to the abuse being issued out in healthy doses to the women married to clergy, simply because of who is inflicting the abuse, upon whom the abuse in being rendered, and where the abuse is taking place. God has made it clear, the responsibility of the church is to preach the gospel of love, and be an example for all to see the fruit of the spirit being manifested in the lives of His sons and daughters. The Bible makes this pointedly clear; "In the last days, God says, I will pour out my spirit on all people. Your sons and daughters will prophecy, your young men shall see visions, your old men will dream dreams. Even on my servants, both men and women, I will pour out my Spirit in those days, and they will prophecy."(Acts 2:17,18 NIV) This passage of scripture clearly indicates God's intention to distribute the ability and responsibility to both men and women to share the Gospel message of love to the world. Women ministers don't cast their husbands aside, or relegate them to servitude roles because they don't seek out, or respond to sexual overtures, when their ministerial success rating hits the roof; men do. Women don't need affirmation or accolades from other men to boost up their morale and inflate their ego on a daily basis; men do. Women don't need a harem or entourage of men to remind them of their outstanding "altogetherness and uniqueness"; men do. Women know how to stay the course when every plan and projections have failed; men crack up. Women are specialists at rising up from the ashes of despair and degradation; men pack up and leave. Women know how to gather up the leavings in the aftermath of a terrible storm, whether a storm of nature or a storm of controversy in the church, and begin to restore order, so that we might begin to start all over again. Many men drop their heads in disgust and despair, and give up. Women seem to be able to adjust and adapt to the circumstances. They are like Timex; they can take a licking and keep on ticking. Some men, however, react to the circumstances; when times are up, they are up; when times are down, they are down. Throughout these pendulum movement of success, status, and circumstances, the clergy wife strives to perform her duty as encourager/comforter to her husband, involve herself in as much activities in the church as she can, so that there will be no lack, and at the same time manage the home, and care for her children. Is this not a commendable task? Is this not worthy of appreciation, honor and respect? Many of these men forget what they have just come through, and who helped them navigate the rough waters of despair until they reached the peaceful lake of success. Why do they forget the softness of safety provided by the loving care of his wife? Why do they forget the daily encouraging words of change, that helped them until change actually came? What makes these men of God forget their covenant spouse of love and trust, to gorge themselves with the forbidden fruit of a younger smile, or the unsolicited praise of a just arrived Jezebel who specializes in feel good rhetoric and promises she can make him even greater, because he deserves the best. And, of course, he agrees, he is entitled to better, even if it hurts his wife.

My Theology of Social Change

My theory of social change starts with getting in touch with revolutionary ideas, asking questions and the ability to confront issues without the need for affirmation or endorsement. My reason for making these theological statements is to address the enormous injustice and patriarchal abuse that continues to invade and prevail in the African American churches and families in this 21st century. My revolutionary ideas came as a result of open and blatant sexual indiscretions committed by male clergy throughout various denominations. My theological perspective has prompted me to engage in ideas that address how women can identify and develop alternative measures in dealing with their pain of betrayal, rejection and confusion. I have questioned, why has the church failed in its mission to uphold moral and ethical standards of character and integrity as God's ambassadors? It has been my responsibility as a marriage and family therapist and clergy to address the dynamics of infidelity and sexual addictions that continue to invade and confine personal lives, and families from actualizing transformational possibilities. After counseling the abused and neglected clergy wives for 30 years, I have decided to become a clarion voice for women who were ready for change and ready for alternatives that would lead them to solutions, closure and celebration. My passion increased as I began to expose, challenge, confront, liberate and transform lives. I realized throughout the 30 years of counseling clergy wives, they were not willing or prepared to confront the injustices that affected all aspects of their social life. Because women have been trained and conditioned to make sacrifices in and out of the home, they were equally trained to repress and sacrifice their needs for the needs of their husbands.

Although clergy wives still have more opportunities for growth, clergy wives are now addressing their concerns and attempting to look for solutions in their dilemma they face in their everyday lives. Back in 1980, women accepted things as they were and showed no interest to challenge male dominance, or challenge their own thought process and belief system. This gradual shift in their belief system was a major contributor in empowering clergy wives to revisit their own theology. I began to realize I was not the only clergy wife that wanted more. We believed that there was more and we began to challenge the patriarchal system for answers and solutions.

For the sake of discussion, what are the crucial realities of women's oppression? Is it the way mothers repeat and foster their generational socializations into the lives of their children? Women are trained from little girls for their eventual roles as wife and mother. The very first toys they are given are dolls, babies, tea sets and toy stoves; these are tools for their socialization. At church, they inherit their "place" from what they see their mothers do. They watch mom's acceptance of her position as what is to be; after all, this is what her mother showed her and her mother before her. In the book of Ruth, we see this generational obedience manifesting itself in Ruth 1:16-18, "And Ruth said, 'urge me not to leave you or to turn back from following you; for where you go, I will go, and where you lodge, I will lodge. Your people shall be my people and your God my God. Where you die, I will die, and there will I be buried. The Lord do so to me, and more also, if anything but death parts me from you. When Naomi saw that Ruth was determined to go with her, she said no more." (AMP) Women are innately responsive to patterns, that which is placed or done before them, they do - men respond to examples. That is why a man in the house is important to a young boy, so he can learn to be a man by following the example of his father. Patterns, however, become molds, and molds can replicate themselves over and over again, if not somehow, broken. Does the role of the culture dictate its ideas and ideals about women's place in the society? How is it possible that, in every major culture, women have been abused in many different ways: physically, emotionally, mentally and economically inferior? If women are ever going to rise above the over arching and incredible pervasiveness in this sexist society, women will need to ask questions, address their concerns as it relates to their need to grow, expand and finally become authentic. Beginning with the therapeutic alliance relationship that builds between clinician and client, this same methodology construct has the same rewards when trust is established in the context of a mentor/mentee relationship and among clergy wives to foster a safe and confidential group setting.

Women have always had the capacity to gel with other women who were ready to share beyond surface generalities and safe genre. In my teaching experience, my joy was to set the climate and parameters of openness, fidelity and solidarity in an attempt to develop a context of empowering and liberating clergy wives to move forward. Moving forward is a participatory process that enables women to see themselves doing what they never imagined would evolve for them. They have always accepted their plight as "the way things are." 30 years later, 40% of the younger clergy wives are evolving into independent thinkers. The other 60% continue to fear change, the fear of losing their clergy wife status and the fear of being alone and managing life on her own. 25% of these women have never worked and the other 25% lack clerical or professional skills to make it on her own.

Theological and Psychological Implications

Clergy wives have begun to address their empowerment and transformational issues by exploring their alternatives and becoming proactive in planning effective strategies to effectively change their lives.

What is the price that clergy wives pay for open secrets which affects the core of low self-esteem? What are the theological and psychological aspects that allow clergy husbands to diminish their wives socially to become objects rather than subjects? From my vantage point, as a result of counseling clergy wives for the past 30 years, these women never focused their personal lives as a priority for success. African American clergy wives have always responded to the success and status of their husband's achievements and visible accomplishments. Clergy wives typically respond to the needs of their husbands due to the impact of racism and discrimination that affects the psychological core of their husband's insignificance and place in his society. African American clergy wives also take responsibility for what goes wrong in the family and the husbands take the responsibility for blaming the wife for what goes wrong in the church.

Women on the other hand, do not require the validation and recognition their husbands need since their success and accomplishments come in a variety of ways. Her validation comes through her relationships, it comes from bringing forth life through childbirth, it also comes from molding, shaping and impacting lives. These are the engines that hold African American women into their comfort zone of significance. These are the same women who hold professional positions, earn good salaries; dress well, yet their motivation is primarily centered around the family and their church world. In the introduction to the setting (page 5), I used Cathy to illustrate a prominent clergy wife, educated, groomed and manicured well, yet Cathy is typically the majority of clergy wives who support their husband's vision and dreams. This is how women become objects instead of subjects. It has been determined statistically that men are more goal oriented than women. They respond to positions, offices, and personal accomplishes as something they have earned for themselves. Where as women take on the responsibility for the whole family unit. African American communities have accepted the model; men are the head, where women are the eyes and sensitivity of every home. As a result, African American clergy wives assume responsibility for keeping the family unit together, even if they have to absorb shock, shame, humiliation and personal degradation of themselves. In so doing, they exist in a sub-social paradigm with the hope that it will eventually become better because her husband will realize that it is she that he loves. These imbalanced relationships are usually masked in the public persona because the husband is gifted at this profession. But in the privacy of the closed door, the mask comes off because he has determined the security of her position as his wife is important enough for her to protest so she must continue the charade. The woman must learn to smile for the public even though she's bruised, devalued and hurt, often to the point of being numb to the actual reality of her circumstances. Men learn how to play the public game well. Success is the engine that generates their continuance in the games he plays. To the man, covering up, scheming, living divisively is just the necessary conduct for his double life. The woman, on the other hand, will eventually reach the point where she can no longer tolerate being the public partner and the private doormat. Where as it's against her nature to publicly overthrow and renounce her abusive spouse. The maintenance of her mental health and the demands placed on her by the significance of her self-worth will eventually activate a place for survival. It might start with a sister-to-sister revelation. It could begin by her returning to work or to school to complete or add to her education. It could begin by her accepting a position in the school district or the denomination that they belong to. She must eventually take on a role that promotes herself as "I and me" rather than "He and us."

There is much work to accomplish in empowering clergy wives to become who they were meant to be. A great deal of effort from various meetings for clergy wives, has challenged and empowered clergy wives to operate out of the box, out of the patriarchal system and overcoming male dominance. It is not the intention of the organization to authenticate women's Lib or to overthrow the men of God in their roles as fathers and leaders. It is, however, the intention of these meetings to authenticate and celebrate clergy wives so that they may operate freely in their gifts, talents and abilities without tension, without male dominance and without theological dogma.

There are, however, several faith communities who continue to hold fast to the traditional and conservative posture that resembles legalism, sexism and patriarchal dominance.

In 1997, my husband and I left an organization that resembled legalism, sexism and patriarchal dominance. We left this embedded theology to enjoy liberation through a deliberative theology that gives credence to ancient historical and cultural background when exegeting, examining and interpreting the word of God effectively. We could no longer stay in an inhibiting environment where God's directed skills, training and gifts could not be used. This attitude and myopic vision of leadership in the organization where we were born, made it impossible for us to stay. Therefore, my husband heeded the call from God to launch out into the deep and cast our nets on the other side. It is on the other side where the harvest of fresh revelation revealed and freedom from limiting traditions and dogma can be found.

A Season of Joy: A Healing Message for All Women

What Do You Do In The Meantime?

CHAPTER EIGHT

A Season of Joy: A Healing Message for All Women

What Do You Do In The Meantime

Facilitator: Rev. Phyllis E. Carter

The objective of this message is designed to endorse, empower and transform women's lives in accepting their window of opportunity by denouncing tradition, patriarchal apartheid and embracing liberation. In the first book of Samuel, first chapter, Hannah portrayed a symbol of liberation by becoming

1) An agent of change
2) Accepting the main event of her life (seizing the moment)
3) Accepting the ability to confront and challenge her adversarial <u>crises</u> in the midst of a patriarchial and sexist society.
4) An agent of change - Hannah was a trailblazer, one who no longer suppressed her pain of rejection, displacement and her pain of barrenness. She wanted more and did something about it. She rose up and

moved beyond her social construct of gender, oppression and sexism to a place of liberation.

5) Hannah acknowledged the scene of her main event. The fear of facing a main event is a tremendous challenge for many clergy wives to consider. I challenged the women to face their fears and anxieties as they approach the main events of their lives in an effort to raise their consciousness to begin to experience liberation and empowerment.

6) Hannah did not forfeit her right to confront and challenge her main event, just because of her cultural and social construct that limited her chances to survive alone. Hannah ended up making critical choices for herself without the support of others.

Whenever I present this message in the form of a workshop, women are given an opportunity to ask questions and comment on their reflections. The overall response to the presentation was always an eye opener. Many women saw their own lives flash before them in many ways as they each dissected the detail situations in Hannah's experience. They could each relate to the opportunity to revisit, contemplate and redefine their own authenticity. One clergy wife commented, she never realized how the patriarchial system diminished, perpetrated oppression and dehumanized women like Hannah, just because she was a woman. She further elaborated, the 21st century women have and still experience the same depraved abuse and oppression as the women in the 1st century. How ironic, women continue to support the system as co-conspirators in the same patriarchial system, in the church and in the home. There was an overwhelming presence of relief and satisfaction by the women as they disclosed and shared in this forum of clergy wives and clergy women as well.

This presentation equally exposed clergy wives to the fact that what they were going through individually was being experienced by a clergy wife. The fact that there was a mutuality in circumstances opened up the potential for a bonding through sharing, thus creating a strength in knowing I am not alone. This brought about solidarity and empowerment among the women as they each experienced freedom to share their valuable stories.

It was significant because the material was not only information that could be understood, it was applicable and usable to the individual participants. Many seminars and workshops attended by the clergy wives deal with bible courses, church procedures and outlines describing books of the bible. The clergy wives felt like courses that dealt with their issues and problems they had experienced, were very significant and the contribution was valuable because the information shared with them was appropriate for their circumstances. One of the most important things any woman can take home from the convocation is information they did not have before. This paradigm shift can be a major breakthrough in the direction of accomplishing and resurrecting freedom for the clergy wife and from the abusive restrictions of her past.

Continuing Research Agenda

CHAPTER NINE

Continuing Research Agenda

As a result of my research project, I have discovered that clergy divorce has risen substantially over the past decade. For further examination, I will explore additional factors that contribute to the increase of clergy divorce, including spousal abuse. Some of these factors have led to divorce and imprisonment. Case in point, in 2002, the president of a major minister's wives convention visited the California Women's Prison to give support to a clergy wife, who was incarcerated for 26 years to life, for killing her pastor, priest and husband. Leading up to this tragic event was constant emotional, verbal, physical, mental abuse, and eventually drug abuse. The startling reality is her husband is dead today, as a repercussion of his abuse. Through fear, she fought back with murder.

My research project has presented a number of challenging concepts that have the capacity to increase our effectiveness in working with spousal abuse in ministry. The focus for my future clinical work will be in educating and sensitizing the African-American clergy and community to take responsibility for developing strategies for changing our training and service delivery approaches through workshops, lecturers, groups, etc. To this end, further violence against women in the church community can be prevented.

Additionally, church leadership has not been properly trained or prepared, to address the reality that divorce is an option in some clergy families. I have come to the conclusion and realization that church leadership has not realized or addressed, the reality that divorce in clergy families are an option, due to the stereotypical stigma and power symbol created by the patriarchal system. I have discovered the significant increase of clergy divorce throughout the country and in almost all denominations. Although it is not the focus of my paper, however, divorce is an on-going research. I would like to explore the dynamics and the central underlying themes that exist throughout the patriarchal, hierarchical and theological tenets that contribute to violence against women in the African-American church community.

About The Author

We, the site team, have reached a series of consensus evaluations concerning Phyllis E. Carter. As she pursues her doctorate degree, her gifts, talent, and skills become more pronounced.

<u>As a Counselor</u>, Phyllis is extremely professional, direct yet comforting. Her skills are outstanding. Her reputation in this field of endeavor is impeccable.

<u>As an Educator</u>, Phyllis is always well informed, and well prepared. She is seldom caught off guard in the classroom setting. Her students are challenged by her teaching style and always leave her class well informed.

<u>As an Author</u>, Phyllis has published two books, *The Pastor's Rib and His Flock,* published 1979 and *The Silent Sufferers,* published in 1994. She has written countless magazine articles for women's organizations and seminars. Her writing style is warm, understandable, informative, and always on point.

<u>As an Administrator</u>, Phyllis is outstanding. We feel she excels in this area because of her ability to set goals and boundaries. She gives directions clearly, establishes lines of

communication and is outstanding in conflict resolution.

<u>Conference and Seminar Speaker</u>, Phyllis excels in this particular area and is called upon constantly. She receives invitational requests not only from coast to coast, but also internationally. By combining her theological training and counseling skills, her teaching/preaching on inner healing is not only outstanding, it is effective.

<u>As Pastor</u>, Phyllis has proven to be very effective. As a result of her husband's decline in health, she has become a very effective ombudsman-assistant to him. She does so very skillfully, endeavoring to lead as he would. She keeps him informed of all decisions; thus he is not threatened of being replaced and the congregation is secure knowing he is still involved in their shepherding.

Our overall assessment of Phyllis conclusively is as follows: Phyllis is a warm caring woman of God. She is competitive, but fair. She is professional, yet down to earth. She is assertive, yet genuinely cares. Phyllis always gives her all in whatever she is involved with.

15-Day Journey and Reflections

It's Time to Move From Your Now to Your Next

15 Day Journal and Reflections

1. Moving Forward

    Moving forward is not an idea, moving forward is a decision. Make a decision to let go of your past hurts and make a decision to let go of the people who rejected and abandoned you. Your destiny is in front of you and all your pain is behind you.

    Moving forward is impossible without the principle of forgiving, forgetting and releasing God to do His best work in you.

Scripture: Phil. 3:13-14; Isa. 43:18-19
Reflections:

_____

_____

_____

_____

_____

_____

2. Celebrating Change

Where there is growth, there is change

Where there is revelation, there is the absence of tradition

Moving forward is the beginning of change

Begin to start loving you, liking you and begin to associate with people who celebrate you.

Are you ready to change?

Are you willing to change?

Are you ready to make the necessary steps to change?

See yourself changed with the help of the Lord

Scripture: Prov. 3:5-7
Reflections:

_____

_____

_____

_____

_____

_____

3. Practice Makes Perfect

Get use to the NEW you

Get use to different locations and venues

Get use to the other side of you, that you have been missing most of your life (your authentic self)

Practice and perform who God said you are, and begin to agree with God's wonderful assessment of you. God knows, more than anyone who you really are and who you will become.

Enjoy your excursion and enjoy your authenticity.

Scripture: Isa 43:18-19
Reflections:

_____

_____

_____

_____

_____

_____

4. Behind the Scenes

Behind the scenes are those areas in your life when God protected, shielded, and concealed the deep pain you experienced in your life. Now that you're ready to move forward, this could be your time (your season) when God exposes you for a public miracle.

Remember, your suffering was not for you alone. Your growth experiences are now for you to reveal and help other women experience, empowerment, and transformational possibilities.

Scripture: Gal. 6:9

Reflections:

_____

_____

_____

_____

_____

_____

5. Intentional Goals

Intentional goals requires determination, cultivation and God's timing.

Monitor your distractions

Monitor your unnecessary activities and, assess who you align yourself with, in order to embrace divine covenant relationships in your refreshing and new beginnings.

What is the next step you need to make to avoid excuses and distractions that hold you back from moving forward.

Scripture: Phil. 3:12-14
Reflections:

_____

_____

_____

_____

_____

6. Your Time Is Now

Are you ready to move from your now to your next? It's all up to you.

Your next will reveal your next assignment. You will then acknowledge you were birthed for greatness and appointed for such a time as this. Remember, everybody will not understand or accept what God is doing in your life because they are not involved in what God is doing in your life. Trying to explain to people what God is doing in your life is a futile task and endeavor. As you begin to release the people in your life that no longer serve in your new capacity, God will put other people in your life who are operating under the same principles of revelation, by stepping up to God's divine intervention. God's process starts with Forgiving, Forgetting, Releasing, Leaving and Becoming. Forgetting your past pain is necessary in order to Release the new directives and new experiences. These new directives and experiences will help you explore new and exciting challenges that you are actually ready to experience, in order to Become what you were born to be; psychologically and theologically whole.

Scripture: Phil. 4:13. I Chron. 4:9-10.
Reflections:

_____

_____

_____

_____

_____

_____

7. Meeting God Through Spiritual Disciplines

Spiritual disciplines bring focus and direction into your life.

Focus and direction is an asset to your growth and development. Schedule yourself with God, you never know when God will show up and set you up for your next visitation of divine revelation.. Present God with your best time, early, free of distractions and open for clarity. Read the book entitled, "Celebrations of Discipline" by Richard J. Foster.

Scripture: Proverbs 3:5-7
Reflections:

_____

_____

_____

_____

_____

_____

8. No More Guilt, No More Shame

Most of our guilt and shame experiences come from scripts and shallow covenants from our past. The people who did not celebrate you for who you were, or the people who unintentionally or intentionally set you up for failure were also victims of their past. Remember, the people who could not celebrate you, did not have anyone to celebrate them as well.

You will never be able to change what has happened or what has been said, but you can change and control where you are going based on your decision to move forward.

Recognize now, that you are not responsible for what was said or what happened to you in the past. You are only responsible for your present thoughts and present actions and present decisions to move forward.

Scripture: Rom. 8:12-14
Reflections:

_____

_____

_____

_____

_____

_____

9. Affirmation, Transformation and Celebration

Now it is your time to receive, accept and affirm who God said you are. It is your season to rejoice and receive all that God has for you. Are you ready? or, do you still need more time to adjust to the new climate and new beginnings that God is ready to reveal to you.

Scripture: I Timothy 1:7
Reflections:

----

10. Free and Empowered

Free and empowered – means you have decided to receive all that God has for you. It also means – you no longer make excuses, or give alibis, for not doing what people anticipate or expect you to do.

Now, you have developed the art of confrontation and setting clear boundaries. Remember, people will continue to expect you to do what you have done most of your life. What a wonderful challenge to now follow God's precepts and examples. ▪

Scripture: Mark 11:24; John 15:7
Reflections:

----

11. Making Room for Others

This new transition will place you with other people that will recognize and respect your talents and abilities. In some cases, the people that you least expect will contribute to your new success in God. Open your heart and experience God's freedom. Believe His Word. Trust His Word. Trust His Love.

You are now well on your way.

Scripture: Prov. 18:16
Reflections:

_____

_____

_____

_____

_____

_____

12. Closing The Door To Past Hurts Once and for All
(Excerpts from "The Silent Sufferers by Phyllis E. Carter)

Here are some of the steps and methods you can use to close the door to your past:

1. Acknowledge the fact that no one but you can close your own door.
2. Read Philippians 1:12:
   "But I would ye should understand, brethen, that the things which happened unto me have fallen out rather unto the furtherance of the gospel."
3. Acknowledge the three levels of spiritual growth.

    a. Getting started: hearing and responding to God.

    b. Making progress: acting on God's Word.

    c. Going on toward perfection. No one reaches perfection, but our goal should be to move in that direction toward a higher maturity level.

4. Understand that everyone controls the handle to his or her door.

5. Open the door to Jesus, for He is standing at the door and waiting with great anticipation to receive you. "Behold, I stand at the door, and knock: if any man hear My voice, and open the door, I will come in to him, and will sup with him, and he with Me." (Rev. 3:20).

6. Close the door to the negative; open the door to the positive.

7. Close the door on your distorted images by being delivered from these distortions. Abolish thoughts such as: *"Because my parents were unavailable and neglected me as a child, then God will neglect me. How can I trust God when I was not able to trust anyone in my life?"* Remember that the Psalmist said: *"The Lord will perfect that which concerned me"* (Ps. 138-8a).

8. Close the door to the old; open the door to the new. "Remember ye not the former things, neither consider the things of old. Behold, I will do a new thing; now it shall spring forth..." (Isaiah 43:18-19).

9. Close the door to your deepest hurt; open the door to your healing.

10. Close the door to your past; open the door to fresh revelation.

Stepping Through The Door of Opportunity

Leave the compartment of your yesterday and then close it tight! You're now standing in fresh anointing – your new day. Now, there's another door in front of you. It's the door of your "shall be", and God will begin to show you what is to come. The door of your "shall be" cannot open until you close and secure the door of your yesterday. Too many people keep the door of their yesterday ajar, and the ghost of the past sneaks into your "new day," preventing them from opening the door to your "shall be." Therefore, you must slam and shut the door of your yesterday and put a final lock on that door.

The new you is changing. The ghost can't get back in: no more hate and bitterness; no more depression and rebellion; no more rejection and getting even. The only thing left is to pull on the door of your "shall be." As Bishop T.D. Jakes says, "Now, you're just one decision, one idea away from your miracle."

Every door has a key, and because God works in levels and seasons, every level has a door called the "door of opportunity." There are seasons of learning, growing and hurting, and you often experience deception and betrayal before you get to your season of victory. *"And let us not be weary in well doing: for in due season we shall reap, if we faint not"* (Gal. 6:9)

Now, when you open the wrong door, close it quickly! Don't linger; you've come too far. Hold tight to your key of destiny.

Finally, you've opened the right door. You're at the right level; you've gone through your seasons; you've gotten your breakthrough; and now you're waiting for your release.

"Nay, in all these things we are more than conquerors through Him that loved us. For I am persuaded, that neither death, nor life, nor angels, nor principalities, nor powers, nor things present, nor things to come, nor height, nor depth, nor any other creature, shall be able to separate us from the love of God, which is in Christ Jesus our Lord." (Romans 8:37-39).

When you can praise God in your wilderness experience, that's what gets God's attention! Always remember that praise is the prerequisite to worship and worship ushers us to our miracles. Blessings and miracles are what you're striving for; that's where you're headed, and that's where God is.

Scripture: Ps. 34:19-22, Ps. 37:5-6
Reflections:

_____

_____

_____

_____

_____

_____

13. Recognizing Your Potential

Your potential and possibilities are now being actualized by you. Revisit #5 – Intentional Goals.

- Make it happen
- Perform your dreams
- Write your vision and make it clear
- Understand, you are living in God's favor. Begin to speak favor into your life for the rest of your life

- Read, "Your Best Life Now" by Joel Osteen

Scripture: Prov. 12:1-2
Reflections:

_____

_____

_____

_____

_____

_____

14. Role Conflict and Role Confusion
(Excerpts from "The Silent Sufferers by Phyllis E. Carter)

Very often, when caught in a role and position that's as visibly spotlighted as a pastor's is, there is that tendency to ignore, forget, or dismiss the fact that you are a person needing affirmation of your personhood, outside of your role or position. Yet how can you affirm your personhood when you're trying to fit in a role that's not clear to you or anyone else? On top of that, what do you do when one of your roles conflicts with another?

In his book, *The Walk-On-Water Syndrome* (1984), Edward B. Bratcher states:

> "Role confusion and role conflict can form an unholy alliance to block fulfillment in ministry. There are ways to respond to these issues in such a fashion that potentially painful experiences will lead to great fulfillment for both clergy and congregation."

Setting biblical priorities and boundaries is critical in activating God's wisdom, God's power, and God's purpose for our lives. Since God never intended for the family to suffer because of the ministry, pastors who are struggling with role confusion and role conflict need to examine their priorities and make sure they line up: God, family, church. When we allow Christ to take the lead, and spend more time in listening to and following His direction, God's proper order and His divine balance will become evident in our lives.

Scripture: Col. 3:1-4, Eph. 5:21, Rom. 12:18-19
Reflections:

_____

_____

_____

_____

_____

_____

15. Pursuing Your Purpose

Identify your authentic goals; these goals will identify your passion.

Write a nice long list of your special attributes and creative abilities and list your personal professional and spiritual goals.

Write a second list, identify the goals you feel you cannot accomplish then try to identify the obstacles or other forces you might feel attribute to the incompletion of your past or present goals.

Remember:

You were born with a purpose
You were born for a purpose
You were born on purpose

Follow your dreams, work on your vision and write the vision and make it clear. Finally, keep a journal of the completion of each of your goals.

Begin to celebrate your achievements and transformational possibilities.

Scripture: Ps. 20:4-5
Reflections:

_____

_____

_____

_____

_____

_____

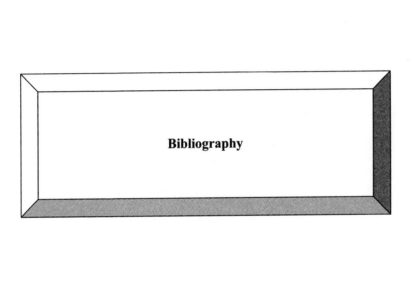

Bibliography

Bibliography

Adams, Carol J. *Woman Battering.* Minneapolis: Fortress Press, 1994.

Aiken, Kenneth T. *Proverbs: The Daily Study Bible Series.* Louisville Kentucky: Westminister John Knox Press, 1998.

Ammons, Linda L. *"Babies, Bath Water, Racial Imagery and Stereotypes: The African-American Woman and the Battered Woman Syndrome."* Wisconsin: Law Review 1003-1004. 1995.

Auld, Graeme A. *The Daily Study Bible Series.*Louisville, Kentucky: Westminster John Knox Press, 1984.

Avery, Bylly. *An Altar of Words: Wisdom, Comfort, and Inspiration for African American Women.* New York: Broadway Books, 1998.

Benyei, Candace R. *Understanding Clergy Misconduct in Religious Systems.* New York: The Haworth Pastoral

Press, Inc, 1998.

Boyd-Franklin, Nancy. *Black Families in Therapy: A Multisystems Approach.* New York: Guilford Press, 1989.

Browne, D. Anne. *You Can Get There From Here: Life Lessons on Growth and Self Discovery for the Black Women.* Orange, New Jersey. 1995.

Carnes, Tony. "Ned Graham's Woes Shake East Gates Ministries." Christianity Today, 1999. 43 No 14 26 D6.

Carter, Phyllis E. *The Silent Sufferers: Understanding The Cross They Bear.* Shippensburg, Pa: Destiny Image Publ., Inc., 1996.

Cashman, Kevin. *Leadership from the Inside Out: Becoming a Leader for Life.* Provo, UT: Executive Excellence Publishing, 1998.

Catherine Clark Kroeger and James R. Beck. *Women, Abuse, and The Bible: How Scripture Can be Used to Hurt or Heal,* Grand Rapids, Michigan: Baker Books, 1996.

Clifford, Richard J. *Proverbs: A Commentary* Louisville, Kentucky: Westminster John Knox Press, 1999.

Collins Hill, Patricia. *Black Feminist Thought.* New York: Routledge, 2000.

David Johnson and Jeff Van Vonderen. *The Subtle Power of Spiritual Abuse.* Minnesota: Bethany House Publ., 1991.

Davis, Ellen F. *Proverbs, Ecclesiastes, and the Song of Songs.* Louisville, Kentucky: Westminster John Knox Press, 2000.

De La Torre, Miguel A. *Reading the Bible from the Margins.* New York: Orbis Books, 2002.

Dempsey Douglass, Jane and James F. Kay. *Women, Gender and Christian Community.* Louisville, Kentucky: Westminster John Knox Press, 1997.

Dobson, Jualyne E. and Cheryl Townsend Gilkes. *Something Within: Social Change and Collective Endurance in the Sacred World of Black Christian Women.* San Francisco: Harper and Row Publishers, Vol 3. 1968.

Douglas, Kelly Brown. *Sexuality and the Black Church.* New York: Maryknoll, Orbis Books, 1999.

Eugene, Toinette M. *Sexuality and Sources for Theological Reflection,* Ed. James B. Nelson and Sandra P. Longfellow Louisville, Kentucky: Westminister John Knox Press, 1994.

Evans, James H., Jr. *We Have Been Believers.* Minneapolis: Fortress Press, 1992.

Exley, Richard. *The Rhythm of Life: Putting Life's Priorities in Perspective.* Tulsa, Oklahoma: Harrison, Inc, 1978.

_____ *Perils of Power:* A division of Harrison House, Inc. Tulsa, Oklahoma, 1988.

Felder, Cain H. *Troubling Biblical Waters*. New York: Orbis Books, 1998.

Foster, Richard J. *Celebration of Discipline: The Path to Spiritual Growth*. New York: San Francisco Harper, 1999.

Fortune, Marie M. *Is Nothing Sacred?* Cleveland. Ohio: United Church Press, 1989.

Franklin, Anderson J. "Therapy With African American Men:" <u>*Families in Society*</u> 73 (June 1992): 351

Gandy, Debrena Jackson. *All the Joy You Can Stand: 101 Sacred Power Principals for Making Joy Real in Your Life*. New York: Crown Publishers, 2000.

Gilkes, Cheryl Townsend. *If It Wasn't for the Women: Black Women's Experience and Womanist Culture in Church and Community*. Maryknoll, New York: Orbis Books, 2001.

_____ *Plenty Good Room: Adaptation in a Changing Black* hurch. The Annals of the American Academy of Political and Social Science. July, 1998.

_____ *The Loves' and Troubles' of African-American Women's Bodies: The Womanist Challenge to Cultural Humiliation and Community Ambivalence*. Maryknoll, New York: Orbis Books, 1993.

Goodrich, Thelma Jean. *Women and Power: Perspectives for Family Therapy*.New York: W. W. Norton & Co., Inc., 1991.

Gordon, D. Fee & Douglas Stuart. *How To Read the Bible for All It's Worth: A Guide to Understanding the Bible.* Grand Rapids, Michigan: Zondervan Publishing Co, 1986.

Harris, Frederick C. *Something Within: Religion in African-American Political Activism.* New York: Oxford University, 1999.

Hooks, Bell. *Teaching To Transgress.* New York: Routledge. 1994.

_____ *Yearning: Race, Gender, and Cultural Politics:* Boston, MA: South End Press, 1994.

Howard W. Stone and James O. Duke. *How To Think Theologically.* Minneapolis: Fortress Press, 1996.

Jacobson, Neil, Ph.D. and John Gottman, Ph.D. *When Men Batter Women: New Insights into Ending Abusive Relationships.* New York: Simon and Schuster, 1998.

Joe E. Trull, & James E. Carter. *Ministerial Ethics.* USA: Broadman & Holman, 1993.

Joel Levey and Michelle Levey. *Living In Balance; A Dynamic Approach For Creating Harmony and Wholeness in a Chaotic World,* Berkeley, CA: Conari Press, 1998.

Johnnette Betsch Cole and Beverly Guy-Shaftall. *Gender Talk: The Struggle for Women's Equality in African American Communities,* New York: One World Ballentine Books, 2003.

Keck, Leander E. *Introduction to the New Interpreter's Bible*, Nashville, TN: Abingdon Press, 1994.

Kidner, Derek. *Proverbs: An Introduction and Commentary.* Downers Grove, Illinois: Inter-Varsity Press, 1964.

Knox, D. H. Spirituality: A Tool in the Assessment and Treatment of Black Alcoholics and Their Families. Alcoholism Treatment Quarterly, (2 (3/4) 1985.

Kornfeld, Margaret. *Cultivating Wholeness.* New York: Continuum, 2000.

Law, Eric H. F. *The Wolf Shall Dwell With The Lamb.* St. Louis, Missouri: Chalice Press, 1993.

Lockhart, Lettie L. *Spousal Violence: A Cross Racial Perspective in Black Family Violence* Lexington, Massachusetts: In Robert L. Hampton (Ed.), 1991.

MacDonald, Lesley. "Clergy Wives Tell of Bashings." Surry Hills, ustralia: *Daily Telegraph,* 1997.

McAdoo, Harriette Pipes. *Black Families.* London: Sage Publications. 1997.

McClain, George D. *Claiming All Things For God. A Guide To Prayer, Discernment, and Ritual For Social Change:* Nashville, TN, Abingdon Press, 1985.

McKim, Donald K. *Westminster Dictionary of Theological Terms.* Louisville, Kentucky: Westminster John Knox Press, 1996.

Monica McGoldrick, John K. Pearce and Joseph Giordano. *Ethnicity and Family Therapy.* New York: The Guilford Press, 1982.

Nobles, W. W. *Africanity: Its Role in Black Families. The Black Scholar.* 5. 1980.

Sanders, Cheryl J. *Hope and Empathy: "Toward an Ethic of Black Empowerment" The Journal of Religious Thought,* Howard University School of Divinity (Vol. 52, Number 2, and Vol. 53, Number 1) 1996.

Sanderson Streeter, Carole, "Whatever Happened to His Wife." *Christianity Today,* 3 April 1995. V. 39.

Smith, Paul P. *Empowering Ministry.* Louisville, Kentucky: Westminster John Knox Press. 1996.

Staples, Robert. *Black Masculinity: The Black Males' Role in American Society.* San Francisco, CA: Black Scholar Press, 1982.

Vandergrift, Nicki Verploegen. *Organic Spirituality: A Six-fold Path for Contemplative Living.* New York: Maryknoll Orbis Books, 2000.

Warhola, Debbie. "Clergymen's Wife of the 90's is Independent-Minded Yet Supportive." Knight Ridder/ Tribune News Service. 27 March 1996, p. 327, k 0550.

West, Cornel. *Race Matters.* New York: Vintage Books, 1993.

White, Evelyn C.. *Chain, Chain, Change: For Black Women in Abusive Relationships.* Seattle, Washington: Seal Press. 1985.

Wilson, P.B. *Liberated Through Submission: The Ultimate Paradox* Minneapolis: Augsburg, 1989.

Wimberly, Edward P. *Counseling African-American Marriages and Families.* ouisville, Kentucky: Westminster John Knox Press, 1997.

Wink, Walter. *The Powers That Be: Theology For A New Millennium,* New York: Galilee Doubleday , 1998.

For more information and book orders, please contact

Refuge Apostolic Church of Christ
106 Broadway
Freeport, N.Y. 11520
Phone: (516) 868-0400
Fax: (516) 223-9068

Email Address: refugefreeport@aol.com

To **Order** copies of this book

The Silent Sufferers

<u>Author</u>: **Dr. Phyllis E. Carter**

$17.00 + 2.50 (s&h)

By phone:

(516) 868-0400

By fax:

(516) 223-9068

By mail:

Mail to address below:

Dr. Phyllis E. Carter

106 Broadway

Freeport, NY 11520

Make all checks payable to Dr. Phyllis E. Carter

Other items available are: Sermons — $10.00 (Audio CD)

1. *I Missed The Line Up but I Made The Setup*
2. *I Was Known by My Pain but Now I'm Known By My Name*
3. *I Got You Where I Need You*

Name: _____

Address: _____

_____

Phone: _____

Email: _____

Credit Card #: _____

Card Type: _____ Exp. Date: _____

Feel free to email Dr. Phyllis E. Carter at refugefreeport@aol.com for more further details.

TINA BAKER MINISTRIES, INC.
REV. TINA L. BAKER

BOOKS

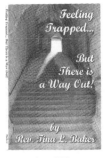

THE PREACHED WORD
Available in audio CD and Audio Cassette Tape

PART I & PART II
AVAILABLE ON DVD AND VIDEO
FEELING TRAPPED? THERE IS A WAY
OUT! & THE CONNECTION

Through this ministry, we want to help you be the best that you can be. Receive deliverance, restoration, and hope. Through the ministry of books, music, play, and preachments – there is something here just for you. We want to help you in any way we can, and we pray that our website (www.tinabaker.org) will bring you closer to God and His good plan for your life. Be empowered to walk away from repeat offenders and embrace the promises of God for your life. Take the slump out of your posture and lift your head up high. Recognize who you are in God. Become who you were born to be.

TINA BAKER MINISTRIES, INC.

106 Broadway   Freeport, NY 11520   USA   Phone: (516) 868.0400   Alt Phone: (516) 244.4210   Fax: (516) 223-9068

Email: tina@tinabaker.org   Website: www.tinabaker.org

TINA BAKER MINISTRIES, INC.

TINA BAKER MINISTRIES, INC.
106 Broadway ~ Freeport, NY 11520
Phone: 516.868.0400 or 516-244-4210
www.tinabaker.org * tina@tinabaker.org

Quantity	Item	Description	Unit Price	Total
	Book	Feeling Trapped but there is a way out!	13.00	
	DVD/VIDEO	**PLAY: Feeling Trapped? THERE IS A WAY OUT!!!! PART I**	20.00	
	DVD/VIDEO	**PLAY: Feeling Trapped? THE CONNECTION PART II**	20.00	
	Book: Audio CD	Feeling Trapped but there is a way out	20.00	
	Book	Become Who You Are Born To Be	15.00	
	Preachment: Audio CD	Behind Enemy Lines	10.00	
	Preachment: Audio CD	Become Who You Are Born To Be	10.00	
	Preachment: Audio CD	Can You Hear Me Now? *Good*	10.00	
	Preachment: Audio CD	I Missed the Line Up But I Made The Set Up	10.00	
	Preachment: Audio CD	Who Said Junior Had To Be A Boy?	10.00	
	Preachment: Audio CD	Who's Your Baby Daddy	10.00	
	Preachment: Audio CD	The Scarecrow Has No Power	10.00	
	Preachment: Audio CD	I'm Moving With or Without You	10.00	
	Preachment: Audio CD	This was no accident, it had to happen this way	10.00	
	Preachment: Audio CD	Don't Count Me Out!	10.00	
	Preachment: DVD	Conference: Life Without Limits **Speaker**: Pastor Michel White-Haynes	20.00	
	Preachment: DVD	Conference: Life Without Limits **Speaker**: Dr. Wanda Turner	20.00	
	Preachment: Audio CD	**Life Without Limits –** Don't get stuck in your step	10.00	
2 cd's (Series)	*Preachment:* Audio CD	Focus On The Family Series (comes w/ 4 cd's)	30.00	
		Shipping & Handling $2.50 per item	TOTAL	

All messages are also available in audio cassette tape for $5.00

Check/Money Order: Please make all check payable to
Tina Baker Ministries and mail it to – 106 Broadway – Freeport, NY 11520